Discovering

the

C&O Canal

and adjacent Potomac River

D0915849

Discovering
the
C&O Canal
and adjacent Potomac River

Mark D. Sabatke

Discovering the C&O Canal
and adjacent Potomac River
by Mark D. Sabatke

Published by:
Schreiber Publishing Inc.
PO Box 4193
Rockville, Maryland 20849
800-296-1961

e-mail: schreiberpublishing@comcast.net

Designed, by Mark D. Sabatke

Printed in the United States Of America

Library of Congress Cataloging-in-Publication Data

Sabatke, Mark D.
    Discovering the C & O Canal and adjacent Potomac River / Mark D. Sabatke.
        p. cm.
    Includes index.
    ISBN 978-0-88400-331-1 (pbk.)
    1. Chesapeake and Ohio Canal (Md. and Washington, D.C.)--Guidebooks. 2.
Chesapeake and Ohio Canal National Historical Park--Guidebooks. 3. Potomac
River Valley--Guidebooks. 4. Outdoor recreation--Chesapeake and Ohio Canal (Md.
and Washington, D.C.)--Guidebooks. 5. Outdoor recreation--Chesapeake and Ohio
Canal National Historical Park--Guidebooks. 6. Outdoor recreation--Potomac
River Valley--Guidebooks. I. Title. II. Title: Discovering the C and O Canal
and adjacent Potomac River.

F187.C47S23 2007
975.2'94--dc22

                                    2007010390

Acknowledgments

Thank You to the following individuals for your collaborative efforts and assistance:

Rick McMullan and family, and Fred King
for access to their wonderful photo libraries and photo captions

Kathy Bilton, Charles Danforth, Jason Robertson, Mary Scott
for their feature articles of special interest

and special thanks to Bettye P. Doherty
for the historic 1939 Trails of the Potomac Valley *print.*

Thank You to the following groups, organizations, and individuals for contributing multiple images and/or content, helping make this book possible:

Jim Atanasoff Photography	*Photos*	*http://members.fortunecity.com/violetpink/contents.html*
Kathy Bilton	*Wildflowers*	*http://www.fred.net/kathy/canal.html*
BSA Troop 1, Charlotte, NC	*Photos, Captions*	*http://community.charlotte.com/realcities/troop1*
BSA Troop 108, Leitersburg, MD	*Photos, Captions*	*http://troop108.homestead.com*
BSA Troop 529, Gibraltar, PA	*Photos, Captions*	*http://www.529gibraltar.org/t529*
BSA Troop 660, Wilmington, DE	*Photos, Captions*	*http://www.udel.edu/hodson/scouts/troop660.htm*
BSA Troop 967, Harve de Grace, MD	*Photos, Captions*	*http://www.home.iximd.com/~msallen/home.htm*
BSA Troop 1970, Reston, VA	*Photos, Captions*	*http://www.troop1970.org/*
Canal Place Preserv. & Dev.	*Summary, Photos*	*http://www.canalplace.org/*
City of Cumberland, MD	*Summary, Photos*	*http://ci.cumberland.md.us/*
Charles Danforth	*Climbing*	*http://www.pha.jhu.edu/~danforth/climb/index.html*
Jim Emery Photography	*Photos, Captions*	*http://www.jimemery.com/*
Fred King	*Photos, Captions*	*http://nursing.cua.edu/candoc/*
Rick McMullan	*Photos, Captions*	*http://www.mcmullans.org/canal/*
Maryland Dept. Natural Resources	*Summary, Photos*	*http://www.dnr.state.md.us/*
Montgomery Sycamore Club	*Summary, Photos*	*http://www.sycamoreisland.org/index.htm*
Nation Park Service	*Summary*	*http://www.nps.gov/*
Rag Tag Rangers	*Photos, Captions*	*http://www.ragtag.org/*
Jason Robertson	*Kayaking*	*http://www.americanwhitewater.com/*
Rocky Gap Resort	*Summary, Images*	*http://www.rockygapresort.com/*
Mart Scott @ Birding America	*Birding*	*http://www.birdingamerica.com/*
Westmar Tours	*Summary, Photos*	*http://www.wstmr.com/*
Dave Winer	*Photos, Captions*	

To the many unnamed Canal-Goers who have contributed to this book, too many to list on one page: This book is really about your discoveries and experiences at the C&O Canal. Thanks to all of you for sharing your experiences.

About This Book

This book is about discovering the natural wonders, the wildlife, and the many activities available at the C&O Canal National Historical Park and the adjacent Potomac River, and all of the wonderful trails, parks, and public lands adjoining or crossing the C&O Canal. The opportunity for adventure and discovery is everywhere; this book will help you plan and experience your C&O Canal and Potomac adventures in new and different ways. This book will help you see the C&O as you have not seen it before.

Specific information provided within this book, i.e. campsite rates, etc. is given as general reference only and may change at any time. Other general and specific information has been compiled from hundreds of different sources, and is presumed to be accurate. Wherever practical information has been corroborated.

The book is divided into three sections:

- *General information on the C&O Canal*
  A brief history and chronology; The locks, aqueducts, and canal boats; Park Service "Hiker/Biker" campsites, private campgrounds, National Park Service C&O Canal Visitor Centers, primary private concessions along the canal, a 4-page mile-by-mile Resources and Services chart, and maps of the canal and its surrounding area.

- *The C&O Canal National Historical Park, a pictorial mile by mile tour*
  The C&O has been divided into thirteen sections of 10 to 20 miles each, as defined by major landmarks and/or locations. Each section starts with a brief overview of the major features and attractions available, points of interest, and boat ramp locations. The pages that follow provide a near mile-by-mile photo tour of the canal sections and its features, activities, and wildlife.
    The C&O ends in Cumberland, Maryland, but the adventures continue. Comprehensive abridged profiles of the major east coast trails crossing or terminating at the C&O are provided. This extensive network of trails provides hiking and camping opportunities in the National and State Parks network throughout Pennsylvania, and interconnects the 2,167-mile Appalachian Trail which traverses the Appalachian Ridge from Georgia to the state of New York.

- *Activities for the C&O and Potomac River region*
  Birdwatching, wildlife, wildflowers, plants and trees, endangered species, outfitters and guides, kayaking, fishing, Maryland mountain biking and ORV trails locations of the region, organizations, clubs, and groups of the C&O Canal and Potomac River. In short, this book can help you get the most from your canal-related experiences and interests.

Note: Whites Ferry or White's Ferry? While Harpers Ferry never seems to carry an apostrophe, all other place names along the C&O Canal sometimes do and sometimes don't. For the sake of consistency, we opted for the apostrophe throughout.

Contents

How the C&O Canal Began

Before it was a national park, the Chesapeake & Ohio (C&O) Canal was one of a network of American canals dug during the late 18th and early 19th centuries to form water highways for commercial trade. These canals played an essential role in developing the North Central territory into states of the union while providing the coastal states with raw materials and fuel for rapid growth.

The C&O Canal is a 184-mile-long National Historical Park. It begins in Washington, D.C. and follows the Potomac River to Cumberland, Maryland. Construction of the Canal began in 1828 and eventually stopped in 1850 when it reached Cumberland. The original plan was to go much further west, but the competition from railroads had not been foreseen.

The C&O Canal paralleled the unnavigable Potomac River and linked Cumberland, Maryland with the nation's capital, using a system of locks to permit heavily laden coal boats to pass to successively lower levels from the mountains to tidewater. The mule teams that pulled the boats along the canal walked on the towpath, guided by the families of the boat captains. The railroad ran beside the C&O Canal and soon made boat traffic an outmoded system when compared to the speed of rail transport.

The C&O Canal finally began making some profits in the 1870's but at the end of the next decade, a massive flood caused the Canal Company to go into receivership to its rival. The B & O railroad operated the Canal for several decades until another devastating flood in 1924, at which time the Canal was closed for good. The C&O and other American canals could not compete and fell into commercial disuse in the early 20th century.

Locks and Aqueducts

Along the course of its 184 miles, the canal had to climb a little over 600 feet. This was accomplished through a series of 74 liftlocks, each of which would raise or lower a canalboat about 8 feet to the next level of the canal, a procedure which generally took about ten minutes. Besides liftlocks, a number of river feeder and guard locks also had to be constructed. These locks allowed water from the river to flow in and out of the canal as needed.

The guardlocks also served to protect the canal during flood periods. Other structures that had to be built as a part of the canal were culverts and aqueducts. To enable the canal to cross relatively small streams, over 150 culverts were built. The crossing of major streams required the construction of 11 aqueducts.

Cargo and Mules

The boats that plied the Canal typically carried cargoes of coal, flour or grain, and made the trip from Cumberland to Georgetown in four or five days. They used teams of two or three mules, working in six-hour shifts. The canalboats generally had crews of five, often all members of the same family. If there were young children living aboard the boats, they would be tethered to the boat to prevent accidents.

Serious injury or death were rare along the Canal. When they did happen the cause was usually simple lack of attention. The same appears to hold true today, with the Potomac River as the major risk, and with outdoor sports activities rather than hauling cargo the cause.

The Canal Chronology

- 1785   Potomac Company chartered
- 1823   Potomac Company resolved to surrender its charter to a new company
- 1824   C and O Canal Company chartered
- 7/4/28   Ground broken for the C and O Canal
- 1831   Canal completed up to Seneca (Mile 23 area)
- 1833   Segment to Harpers Ferry completed (Mile 60 area)
- 1839   Segment to near Hancock completed (Mile 134)
- 1850   Canal completed as far as Cumberland; decision made not to go farther west
- 1877   Boatmen's strike and devastating flood
- 1889   Major devastating flood causing Canal to go into receivership to B&O Railroad
- 1892   Canal repaired and put back into operation
- 1902   Canal Towage Company established. It tightens canal operations and buys up remaining independently-owned boats, replacing distinctive names with numbers
- 1924   First major flood in 35 years; the ruined Canal closed down permanently
- 1936   Biggest recorded flood in Potomac Valley; bridges at Harpers Ferry and Shepherdstown washed out
- 1938   U.S. Government acquires the derelict Canal from the B and O Railroad for $2 million; historic restoration begins on lower 22 miles
- 1939   The Canal is dedicated as a public park
- 1942   Another major flood undoes restoration work
- 1950   Proposal for parkway to Cumberland along Potomac to be constructed issued by assistant Secretary of the Interior
- 1/3/54   Washington Post editorializes in favor of the proposed parkway construction
- 1/19/54   Justice William O. Douglas writes letter to editor inviting the editor to hike the Canal; the Post writes in a January 21 editorial, "We Accept"
- 3/20/54   Hike begins at Lock 72 and ends in D.C. eight days later, with editors conceding that Canal should be preserved
- 1/23/62   President Eisenhower signs a proclamation to establish the Chesapeake and Ohio Canal National Monument in Maryland (but this does nothing to protect Canal from potential road construction)
- 1/8/71   President Nixon signs an act to establish and develop the C and O Canal National Historical Park, authorizing expansion from about 5,000 acres to over 20,000
- 6/24/72   Hurricane Agnes causes great damage that takes years to repair
- 5/17/77   C and O Canal is dedicated to Justice Douglas
- 11/85   Another very destructive flood, with repairs taking over a year
- 1/19-20/96 Devastating flood

The 75 C&O Canal Locks

Lock #	Mile	Name/Location	Lock #	Mile	Name/Location	Lock #	Mile	Name/Location
1	0.38	Georgetown	26	39.37	Wood's Lock	51	122.59	Big Pool
2	0.42	Georgetown	27	41.46	Spink's Ferry	52	122.89	
3	0.49	Georgetown	28	48.93	Point of Rocks	53	129.96	Irishman's Lock
4	0.54	Georgetown	29	50.89	Catoctin, Lander	54	133.96	
5	5.02	Brookmont	30	55.00	Brunswick	55	134.06	Dam No. 6
6	5.40	Magazine Lock	31	58.01	Weverton	56	136.21	Pearre
7	7.00	Chataqua	32	60.23	Sandy Hook	57	139.22	Sideling Hill
8	8.33	Seven Locks	33	60.70	Harpers Ferry	58	143.96	Orleans
9	8.70	Seven Locks	34	61.57	Goodheart's	59	146.56	
10	8.79	Seven Locks	35	62.33	Dam No. 3	60	149.69	
11	8.97	Seven Locks	36	62.44		61	153.10	
12	9.29	Seven Locks	37	66.96	Mountain	62	154.16	
13	9.37	Seven Locks	38	72.80	Shepherdstown	63	154.48	
14	9.47	Seven Locks	39	74.00	One-Mile Lock	64	154.60	
15	13.45	Six Locks	40	79.41	Sharpsburg	65	- -	Cancelled
16	13.63	Six Locks	41	88.90	Dam 4	66	154.70	
17	13.99	Six Locks	42	89.04		67	161.76	Darkey's Lock
18	14.09	Six Locks	43	92.96		68	164.82	Crabtree's
19	14.17	Six Locks	44	99.30	Williamsport	69	166.44	Twigg's Lock
20	14.30	Tavern Lock	45	107.27	Two Locks	70	166.70	Oldtown
21	16.64	Swain's Lock	46	107.42	Two Locks	71	167.04	Oldtown
22	19.63	Pennyfield Lock	47	108.64	Four Locks	72	174.44	The Narrows
23	22.12	Violette's	48	108.70	Four Locks	73	175.36	North Branch
24	22.82	Riley's Lock	49	108.80	Four Locks	74	175.47	North Branch
25	30.84	Edward's Ferry	50	108.87	Four Locks	75	175.60	The Last Lock

The Eleven C&O Canal Aqueducts

	Span	Arches	Length	Stone	Cut
Seneca Creek	113"	3	33' each	Sandstone	Cut stone
Monocacy River	433"	7	54' each	Quartzite	Cut stone
Catoctin Creek	92'	3	20', 40', 20'	Mostly Granite	Ranged bubble below, cut face rough above Piers.
Antietam Creek	103'	3	28', 40', 28'	limestone	
Conococheague Cr	196'	3	60' each	limestone	Arches, skewbacks, ends of Piers and Abutments cut; rest of facelines are hammerdressed and renged
Licking Creek	90'	1	90'	Limestone	Arches, skewbacks,
Big Tonoloway Cr	66'	1	66'	Limestone	water table, coping,
Sideling Hill Creek	66'	1	66'	Sandstone	and inside of parapet
Fifteen Mile Creek	50'	1	50'	V. Hard Sandst.	are cut; the rest of
Town Creek	60'	1	60'	Limestone	masonry is rubble work
Evitts Creek	70'	1	70'	Limestone	

The Canaller
Chesapeake and Ohio Canal National Historical Park Barge Rides

The National Park Service offers living history boat rides at two locations on the C&O Canal. Park rangers in historical clothing transport passengers back in time to the 1870's as they experience locking through a historic lift lock, and being pulled by mules as rangers describe the history of the canal and the families who worked on it.

The Georgetown

For this 70-minute round-trip at Georgetown Washington, DC, call the Georgetown Visitor Center at 202-653-5190 for information.
Fares: $8.00-adults, $6.00-seniors (62+), $5.00-children (4-14 yrs.), Children 3 & Under Free, School or Youth Groups (age 14 and under) of 10 or more $5.00 per person. Other Groups of 10 or more are charged according to age. Groups (10 or more) may reserve seats on public trips. Special reserved trips are also available.

The Canal Clipper

For this one-hour round-trip at Great Falls, Potomac, MD, call the Great Falls Tavern Visitor Center at 301-767-3714 or 301-299-3613 for information.
Fares: $8.00-adults, $6.00-seniors (62+), $5.00-children (4-14 yrs.), Children 3 & Under Free, School or Youth Groups (age 14 and under) of 10 or more $5.00 per person. Other Groups of 10 or more are charged according to age. Special reserved trips are also available.

Twilight Cruise Schedule

This is a wonderful, romantic experience that is often overlook by the local population. After the cruise, fine dining at the Old Angler's Inn, or in Georgetown, is just minutes away. (Reservations are required for this ride.)
NOTE: There is also an entrance fee charged at Great Falls. It costs $5.00 per vehicle for a three-day pass, and $15.00 for an annual pass. Cyclists and walkers pay $3.00. Golden Age, Golden Eagle, and Golden Access passes are honored. Commercial vehicle fees are: 1-6 people-$25.00, 7-25 people-$40.00, over 25 people-$100.00. Educational groups may apply for an entrance fee waiver.

Hiking and Biking the C&O Canal

Hiking and biking along the towpath are excellent ways to see the park. Hiker-biker campsites are located from Seneca to Cumberland at various intervals (see Camping below). Several park areas have interpretive trails and other hiking opportunities. Trail guides are available at Georgetown, Great Falls Tavern, Williamsport, Hancock Visitor Center, Western Maryland Station Center, and Antietam National Battlefield Park.

Bicycle riding is permitted on the towpath but not the trails. The surface of the towpath varies from excellent to rough due to tree roots, rocks, chuckholes, and weather conditions. Avoid using the towpath for at least two days after heavy rainstorms. Bicyclists should avoid the towpath at Wide Water (Mile 13) near Great Falls. Follow the Berma Rd. on the berm side of the canal at Old Anglers Inn and return to the towpath at the stop lock above Lock 16 (Mile 13.6). Bicyclists should also avoid the towpath between Dam 4 (Mile 84.5) and McMahon's Mill (Mile 88.5). Northbound, take Dam 4 Rd. to Dellinger Rd. to Avis Mill Rd.

Bicyclists should yield right-of-way to pedestrians and horses. Sound devices (bells, horns, etc.) are required, and should be used whenever approaching from the rear. Bicyclists should carry tools and materials for repairing broken chains, flat tires, and spokes. *Helmet laws are in effect in Maryland in Montgomery and Allegany counties.* For a bicycle safety handbook, contact the Maryland Department of Transportation, Bicycle Affairs Coordinator, State Highway Administration, PO Box 717, Baltimore, MD 21203, or call 1-800-252-8776 or 301-333-1663.

Camping the C&O Canal

Fees: $10 fee per site per night for Antietam Creek, McCoy's Ferry, Fifteen Mile Creek, and Spring Gap. Group camping areas at Marsden Tract and Fifteen Mile creek will cost $20 per night. Call Park Headquarters at 301-739-4200 for more information. Parking trailers and pitching tents or other equipment are permitted only at designated sites. Trailer length in drive-in camps may not exceed 20 feet. All wheeled vehicles, except wheelchairs and bicycles, must stay off the grass. As in all park areas, pets at campsites must be on a leash or under other physical control. For the comfort of others, quiet is required between 10 p.m. and 6 a.m.

Boat Ramps to the Potomac River

Major boat ramps to the islands include the Mouth of the Monocacy Boat Launch, Pennyfield Boat Launch, Swain's Lock, and C&O Canal Lock 8. For additional information, contact the Seneca Work Center at (301) 258-7308. Boat Ramps may also be found at: Fletcher's Boathouse mile 3, Seneca Creek mile 23, Edward's Ferry mile 31, White's Ferry mile 35, Dickerson Regional Park mile 39, Noland's Ferry mile 44, Point of rocks mile 48, Dargan Bend mile 65, Mountain Lock Recreational Area mile 67, Antietam Creek Recreation Area mile 69, Snyder's Landing mile 76, Taylor's Landing mile 81, Big Slackwater mile 85, Williamsport mile 99, Four Locks Ranger Station mile 108, McCoy's Ferry mile 110, Hancock, Maryland mile 124, Fifteen Mile Creek Aque-

Hiker/Biker Campsite Locations
(for up-to-date info go to: http://www.nps.gov)

These campsites permit tent camping only. Pump well water and pit toilets are on site. Stay is limited to one night per site per trip. Campsites are at least 1 mile from any parking area.

Location	Name of Site	Location	Name of Site
m.16.6	Swain's Lock	m.110	North Mountain
m.26.1	Horsepen Branch	m.116	Licking Creek Aqu.
m.30.5	Chisel Branch	m.120.3	Little Pool
m.34.4	Turtle Run	m.126.4	White Rock
m.38.2	Marble Quarry	m.129.8	Leopard's Mill
m.42.5	Indian Flats	m.133.6	Cacapon Junction
m.47.6	Calico Rocks	m.139.2	Indigo Neck
m.50.3	Bald Eagle Island	m.144.5	Devil's Alley
m.58.3	Appalachian Trail	m.149.4	Stickpile Hill
m.62.9	Huckleberry Hill	m.154.1	Sorrel Ridge
m.69.6	Antietam Cr. ($10)	m.155.8	Paw Paw (Arbaugh)
m.75.2	Killiansburg Cave	m.157.4	Purslane Run
m.79.6	Horseshoe Bend	m.162.1	Town Creek
m.82.4	Big Woods	m.164.8	Potomac Forks
m.90.9	Opequon Junction	m.169.1	Pigman's Ferry
m.95.2	Cumberland Valley	m.175.4	Irons Mountain
m.101.1	Jordan Junction	m.180.1	Evitt's Creek

Drive-in Campsites Locations
(These sites have primitive facilities only. There are no RV hookups.)

Location	Name of Site & Information
m.110.4	McCoy's Ferry; no water available; boat ramp; rv and tent camping $10/site/night
m.140.9	Fifteen Mile Creek; RV and tent camping $10/site/night; (non-group areas) $20/site/night
m.173.3	Spring Gap; rv and tent camping $10/site/night

Group Camping Locations

m.12	Marsden Tract; permit required (call 301-299-3613); reserved for use by civic and scout organizations $20/site/night
m.68	Antietam Creek $10/site/night
m.140.5	Fifteen Mile Creek; boat ramp; rv and tent camping $10/site/night

All campsites (except the Marsden tract) are on a first-come, first-served basis. One family or one camping unit is allowed for each site. Abandoned or unattended personal property may be impounded.

Campgrounds Near the C&O Canal

Bonds Landing Campground
(Stickpile Hill, Green Ridge State Forest)
Kasecamp Road off Mertens Avenue.
Drive in Camping, fee site, Open all year.

Brunswick Family Campground
Maple Avenue
Brunswick, Maryland 21716
(301) 834-8050
*RV hookups, restaurant, pool.

Maple Treehouse Campground
20716 Townsend Road
Gapland, MD 21779
(301) 432-5585
*Cabins, bathrooms, showers, tent sites,
tree houses, tree cottages.

Hidden Springs Campground
PO Box 190
Flintstone, MD 21530
(814) 767-9676
*Toilets, showers, laundry, store, pool, mini
golf, rec room.

Happy Hills Campground
12617 Seavolt Rd
Hancock, MD 21750-2733
*RV hookup, handicap access, Toilets,
showers, laundry, store, utilities, LP gas,
pool, mini golf, rec hall, pets.

Harpers Ferry Campground
RT 5 Box 1300
Harpers Ferry, WV 25425
1-800-562-9497
* RV hookups, utility hookups, handicap
access, bathrooms, hot showers, playground, TV room, laundry, pets.

Indian Springs Kampgrounds
10809 Big Pool Rd
Big Pool, MD 21711
(301) 842-3336
* RV hookups, handicap access, phones,
laundry, LP gas, pets.

Little Orleans Campground & Park
31661 Green Forest Drive, SE

Little Orleans, MD 21766
(301) 478-2325
* RV hookups, toilets, water, power, sewer,
picnic, store, pool, rec hall.

Snug Harbor Koa Campground
11759 Snug Harbor Ln
Williamsport, MD
301-223-7571, 1-800-562-7607
* RV hookups, utility hookups, bathrooms,
showers, playground, TV room, laundry,
pets.

Spring Valley Campgrounds
14400 Old Oldtown Rd, SE
Oldtown, Maryland 21555
301-478-5295, 301-478-5790
* RV hookups, cabins, store, bait shop, propane.

Safari Camp Grounds
16519 Lappans Rd
Williamsport, MD
301-223-7117

McMahon's Mill Rec Area Campground
7900 Avis Mill Rd
Williamsport, MD 21795-2006
(301) 223-8778

Antietam Hagerstown Kampground
11759 Snug Harbor Lane
Williamsport, MD 21795
301-223-7571
* heated swimming pool, kitchen, game room,
playground, theatre, canoes

Hagerstown / Snug Harbor KOA
11759 Snug Harbor Lane
Williamsport, MD 21795
301-223-7571, 800-562-7607
* RV hookups, utility hookups, bathrooms,
showers, playground, TV room, laundry.

Yogi Bear's Jellystone Park Camp
16519 Lappans Road
Williamsport, MD 21795
301-233-7117, 800-421-7116
* RV hookups, cabins, pool w/slide, propane.

Georgetown Visitor Center

1057 Thomas Jefferson Street, NW
Washington, DC 20007
202-653-5190
8:30 - 4:30 Wednesday - Sunday, closed Dec 25 and Jan 1

Special Programs - Ranger-led walks and talks. Mule-drawn canal boat rides. **Exhibits** - Displays interpret canal history. **Available Facilities** - Restroom and bookshop. **Activities** - Canal boat rides, Hiking, Ranger led tours.

Great Falls Tavern Visitor Center

11710 MacArthur Boulevard
Potomac, MD 20854
301-299-3613 or 301-767-3714
9 – 4:30 Monday - Friday,   9 - 5 Saturday & Sunday,
open Thanksgiving, closed Dec 25 and Jan 1

Special Programs - Ranger-led walks and talks. Mule-drawn canal boat rides. **Exhibits** - Displays and short films interpret canal and local history and the geology of the Great Falls of the Potomac.
There is an entrance fee at the Great Falls area of the canal. It costs $4.00 per vehicle for a three day pass, and $15.00 for an annual pass. Cyclists and walkers pay $2.00. National Park Pass, Golden Age, Golden Eagle, and Golden Access passes are honored. Commercial vehicle fees are: 1-6 people-$30.00, 7-25 people-$45.00, over 25 people-$100.00.
Activities - Canal boat rides, Hiking, Ranger led tours

Brunswick Visitor Center

40 West Potomac Street
Brunswick, MD 21716
301-834-7100
10 - 2 Thursday - Friday, 10 - 4 Saturday and Sunday,
closed December 25, and January 1

Special Programs - Ranger led programs offered on many weekends. Call for more information.
Exhibits - Exhibit interprets canal and local history. Short films also present canal history.
Available Facilities - Restroom.

Sharpsburg C&O Headquarters

Route 34 at the Potomac River, Box 4,
Sharpsburg, MD 21782. 301-739-4200

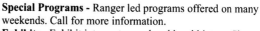

Williamsport Visitor Center

205 West Potomac Street
Williamsport, MD 21795
301-582-0813
9 - 4:30 Wednesday - Sunday
Closed Thanksgiving Day,
Dec. 25, and Jan. 1
Open all year 9 a.m. to 4:30 p.m.

Special Programs - Ranger led programs offered on many weekends and some week-days. Call ahead.
Exhibits - Displays and short films interpret canal and local history and the geology of the Great Falls of the Potomac.
Available Facilities - Restrooms and bookshop. Western
Maryland Station

Hancock Visitor Center

326 East Main Street
Hancock, MD 21750
301-678-5463
9 - 4:30 Friday - Tuesday
Closed Thanksgiving Day, December 25, and January 1
Open all year, hours vary

Special Programs - Ranger led programs offered on many weekends.
Exhibits - Displays and short films interpret canal and local history.
Available Facilities - Restroom and bookshop.

Western Maryland Station at Cumberland

Room 304
13 Canal Street
Cumberland, MD 21502
301-722-8226
Closed Thanksgiving Day, December 25, and January 1
Open 9 - 5 daily, open all year

Special Programs - Ranger led programs offered on many weekends and some weekdays.
Replica canal boat. Excursion steam train nearby. Call ahead.
Exhibits - Displays interpret canal and local history and the geology of the Great Falls of the Potomac. New exhibits and films will open in October.
Available Facilities - Restrooms, snack bar, bookshop.

Primary Concessions on the C&O Canal

Fletcher's Boat House, Inc.
4940 Canal Road, NW
Washington, DC 20007
(202) 244-0461

Open 7 Days per week,
10 a.m. to 6 p.m.

mile 3.1
* Bike and Canoe rentals
* Boat ramp
* Food, drinks, restrooms, gifts, supplies, and more.

Directions: from Georgetown, take M Street, NW (at Key Bridge) 1 mile, left on Canal Road, about 2 miles. From 495 Beltway, exit 39 to DC, about 6 miles.

Great Falls Park
11710 MacArthur Blvd.
Potomac, MD 20854
Snack bar: (301) 301-299-9209

mile 14.1
* Snack bar
* Visitor Center
* Food, drinks, restrooms, gifts, and more.

Open 7 Days per week, 9 a.m. to 5 p.m.

Directions: Exit 39 off Capital Beltway, west on River Road to Potomac Village, left on Falls Road to end, right on MacArthur Blvd., 2 miles to park.

Swain's Lock
Swains Lock Road
Potomac, MD 20854
(301) 299-9006

Open 7 Days per week,
10 a.m. to 6 p.m.

mile 16.6
* Bike and Canoe rentals
* Guided Activities:
Rock Climbing, Canoeing, Kayaking, Rafting, Caving, Mountain Biking, and more.

Directions: Exit 39 off Capital Beltway, west on River Road toward Potomac. Two miles past Potomac Village, left on Swain's Lock Road, to end.

Seneca / Riley's lock
Camp OuterQuest
13015 Riley's Lock Road
Seneca, MD 20837
www.TeamOuterQuest.com

mile 22.8
* Bike and Canoe rentals
* Guided Activities:
Rock Climbing, Canoeing, Kayaking, Rafting, Caving, Mountain Biking, and more.

(3011) 258-1914 * 1-(800) 51-KAYAK
Open 7 Days per week, 10 a.m. to 6 p.m.

Directions: Exit 39 off Capital Beltway, west on River Road past Potomac to Seneca. Left at stoplight, to end.

White's Ferry Store
24801 White's Ferry Road
Dickerson, Maryland 20842
301-349-5200

mile 35.5
* Bike and Canoe rentals
* Boat ramp
* Food, drinks, restrooms, gifts, supplies, and more.

Rec. facilities and Store open:
Friday - Sunday 6 a.m. to 8 p.m.
Monday - Thursday 6 a.m. to 7 p.m.
The ferry operates from 5 a.m. to 11 p.m. daily

Directions: NW on Route 28, left on Route 107 to Poolesville, left on White's Ferry Road, west about 6 miles; South on Route 109 to Poolesville, right White's Ferry Rd.

Barron's C&O Museum and Country Store
PO Box 356
Sharpsburg, MD 21782
(301) 432-8782

mile 76.6
* Food, drinks, gifts, supplies, and more.

Open 9-5 Saturday and Sunday, year-round.
Groups: Call for weekday appointments and history talks.

Directions: from Frederick, take I-70 West to Alt. Rte. 40 (less than 4 miles). Follow 40 west about 10 miles to Boonesboro. Left on Rte. 34. Enter Sharpsburg about 6 miles further, turn right on any street in center of town, and turn left on Snyder's landing Road after just one or two or three blocks. Barron's is just about a mile down, on the right (just past the C&O Canal parking lot).

Canal Place
13 Canal Street
Cumberland, MD 21502
(301) 724-3655   Toll Free: 800-989-9394

From I-68 Westbound: Take Exit 43-C, Downtown. At the bottom of the exit ramp, turn left onto Harrison Street. Continue to the traffic signal at Mechanic & Harrison Streets. Go straight ahead into the WMRS parking lot.

From I-68 Eastbound: Exit 43-C, Downtown. At the bottom of the exit ramp, turn left onto Queen City Dr. Go to the first traffic signal and turn left onto Harrison Street. Continue to the traffic signal at Mechanic & Harrison Sts. Go straight ahead into the WMRS parking lot.

Visitor information is available on the second floor of the Western Maryland Railway Station at the Allegany County Convention & Visitors Bureau Visitor Center.
C&O CanalFest
Saturday & Sunday, Mid-May

MILE MARKER RESOURCES AND SERVICES CHART

MILE	POINTS OF INTEREST	Food	Water	Telephone	Restrooms	Parking	Picnic	Camping	Boat Ramp	Motel	Rentals
000.0	Georgetown: Outdoor Waterfront Cafes.	✓	✓	✓	✓	✓	✓			✓	
000.0	Thompson's Boat Center: Bicycle rentals.								✓		✓
003.1	Fletcher's Boathouse: Snack Bar. Rentals.	✓	✓	✓	✓	✓	✓		✓		✓
003.6	Capital Crescent Trail to Bethesda, MD.										
004.0	Chain Bridge: River crossing to Virginia.					✓					
004.7	Maryland State Line										
005.8	Little Falls Pumping Station										
007.5	Cabin John Bridge										
008.3	Lock 8						✓		✓		
009.3	Capital Beltway (I-495)										
010.4	Carderock Recreational Area		✓		✓	✓	✓				
012.0	Marsden Tract Campground (regist., fee)							✓			
012.6	Widewater Detour: Old Angler's Inn.	✓	✓	✓	✓	✓					
013.0	Bill Goat Hiking Trail: Entrance: No Bikes										
013.4	200 Yard Rocky Breach: Carry Bikes.										
013.7	Widewater Bicycle Detour										
013.8	Bill Goat Hiking Trail: No Bikes										
013.9	Mather Gorge Overlook										
014.0	Great Falls Overlook: No Bikes										
014.3	Great Falls Tavern Visitor Center	✓	✓	✓	✓	✓	✓		✓		
016.6	Swain's Lock: Bike, Canoe Rentals	✓	✓	✓	✓	✓		✓	✓		✓
019.6	Pennyfield Lock					✓			✓		
020.0	Dierssen Wildlife Sanctuary										
021.0	Blockhouse Point cliffs										
022.0	Violette's Lock					✓					
022.8	Seneca, Seneca Cr. Aque., Riley's Lock		✓	✓	✓	✓			✓		✓
026.0	Horsepen Branch H/B campsite		✓				✓	✓			
027.2	Sycamore Landing								✓		
027.2	McKee-Beshers Wildlife Area										
030.5	Chisel Branch H/B campsite		✓				✓	✓			
030.8	Edward's Ferry Boat Ramp: to Poolesville			✓		✓			✓		
031.9	Broad Run Trunk Aqueduct: (Ruins)										
034.5	Turtle Run H/B campsite		✓					✓			

Legend:

⑪ = Food 🔅 = Water 📞 = Telephone 🚻 = Restrooms 🅿 = Parking
🏕 = Picnic ⚠ = Camping 〰 = Boat Ramp 🏨 = Motel Ⓡ = Rentals

C&O CANAL RESOURCES AND SERVICES CHART

MILE	POINTS OF INTEREST	Food	Water	Telephone	Restrooms	Parking	Picnic	Camping	Boat Ramp	Motel	Rentals
035.5	White's Ferry: Ferry Access to Leesburg.	●	●	●		P			●		R
038.1	Marble Quarry H/B campsite		●					▲			
039.6	Dickerson Conservation Area					P					
041.0	PEPCO Dickerson Plant										
042.1	Monocacy Aqueduct					P			●		
042.4	Indian Flats H/B campsite		●					▲			
044.0	Noland's Ferry					P			●		
047.6	Calico Rocks H/B campsite		●					▲			
048.2	Point of Rocks, MD: Access VA. Stores	●	●	●	●	P		▲	●		
050.3	Bald Eagle Island H/B campsite		●					▲			
050.8	Lander Lock					P					
051.5	Catoctin Creek Aqueduct (Ruins)										
054.0	Brunswick Family Campground (RV's Only)						⛱	▲			
055.0	Brunswick, MD - Route 17/287 Bridge	●	●	●	●	P	⛱		●	●	R
055.0	C&O Canal History & Railroad Museums					P					
058.0	Appalachian Trail joins Towpath					P					
058.0	Weverton - Casper W. Weaver House										
060.2	Harpers Ferry Youth Hostel 301-834-7652	●	●	●	●	P		▲		●	
060.2	Sandy Hook, MD			●							
060.7	Harpers Ferry, WV	●	●	●	●	P	⛱	▲		●	R
060.7	Comfort Inn: Harpers Ferry, WV	●	●	●	●	P		▲		●	
061.3	Maryland Heights Hiking Trail: No Bikes					P					
062.3	Feeder Dam 3, Guard Lock 3							▲			
062.9	Huckleberry Hill H/B campsite		●					▲			
064.9	Dargan Bend Recreation Area					P	⛱	▲	●		
067.0	Mountain Lock Recreation Area					P	⛱		●		
069.3	Antietam Aqueduct										
069.4	Antietam Creek Recreation Area: Fee		●		●	P	⛱	▲	●		
072.7	Sharpsburg, MD	●	●	●	●	P	⛱	▲		●	
072.8	Route 34 Bridge: Shepherdstown.	●	●	●	●	P				●	R
072.8	Bavarian Inn: Shepherdstown, WV	●	●	●	●	P				●	
075.3	Killiansburg Campground H/B campsite		●					▲			
075.7	Killiansburg Cave										

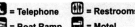

● = Food   ● = Water   ● = Telephone   ● = Restrooms   P = Parking
⛱ = Picnic   ▲ = Camping   ● = Boat Ramp   ● = Motel   R = Rentals

C&O CANAL RESOURCES AND SERVICES CHART

MILE	POINTS OF INTEREST	SERVICES AVAILABLE
076.6	Snyder's Landing Boat Ramp	Food, Water, Boat Ramp
076.6	Jacob Rohrbach Inn: Sharpsburg, MD	Food, Water, Telephone, Restrooms, Parking, Motel, Rentals
076.7	Barron's C&O Canal Museum and Store	Food, Water
079.9	Horseshoe Bend H/B campsite	Water, Camping
081.0	Taylor's Landing Boat Ramp	Boat Ramp, Rentals
082.5	Big Woods H/B campsite	Water, Camping
084.4	Dam #4 (Bike Detour): Use on Road Detour.	Parking, Picnic, Boat Ramp
085.7	Big Slackwater	Picnic, Boat Ramp
088.1	McMahon's Mill (Bike Detour)	Food, Water, Telephone, Parking, Picnic
090.9	Opequon Junction H/B campsite	Water, Camping
095.2	Cumberland Valley H/B campsite	Water, Camping
098.5	I-81 Overpass	
099.3	Williamsport, MD: Stores and Restaurants	Food, Water, Telephone, Restrooms, Parking, Boat Ramp, Motel, Rentals
099.3	Lock 44	
099.7	Cushwa Basin	Food, Water, Restrooms, Parking, Boat Ramp, Motel, Rentals
099.5	Conococheague Aqueduct	
101.2	Jordan Junction H/B campsite	Camping
106.8	Feeder Dam #5	
107.4	Two Locks	
108.6	Four Locks Ranger Station	Water, Telephone, Boat Ramp, Camping, Boat Ramp
110.0	North Mountain H/B campsite	Water, Camping
110.4	McCoy's Ferry Recreation Area	Parking, Picnic, Camping, Boat Ramp
112.4	Fort Frederick State Park	Food, Water, Telephone, Restrooms, Parking, Camping, Boat Ramp
112.5	Big Pool (East End)	
114.0	Big Pool (West End)	Telephone, Parking
116.0	Licking Creek Aqueduct	Water, Camping
116.0	Licking Creek H/B: Subject to Traffic Noise.	Water, Camping
120.4	Little Pool H/B: Subject to Traffic Noise.	Water, Camping, Boat Ramp
123.0	Tonoloway Creek Aqueduct	
124.1	Tuscarora Trail to Pennsylvania	
124.1	Hancock, MD: Stores, Restaurants	Food, Water, Telephone, Restrooms, Parking, Camping, Boat Ramp, Motel, Rentals
124.5	Little Tonoloway	Food, Water, Parking, Boat Ramp, Rentals
126.4	White Rock H/B campsite	Water, Camping

Legend:
- = Food
- = Water
- = Telephone
- = Restrooms
- = Parking
- = Picnic
- = Camping
- = Boat Ramp
- = Motel
- = Rentals

C&O CANAL RESOURCES AND SERVICES CHART

MILE	POINTS OF INTEREST	Food	Water	Telephone	Restrooms	Parking	Picnic	Camping	Boat Ramp	Motel	Rentals
127.4	Round Top Cement Mill										
129.2	Leopard's Mill H/B campsite		●					▲			
131.3	Cohill Station								●		
133.6	Cacapon Junction H/B campsite		●					▲			
134.0	Dam No. 6; Lock 55										
134.2	Polly Pond										
136.6	Sideling Hill Creek Aqueduct										
139.2	Indigo Neck H/B campsite		●					▲			
140.8	Little Orleans	●	●	●	●	P	●	▲	●		
140.8	Fifteenmile Creek Recreation Area: Fee	●	●	●		P		▲	●		R
140.9	Fifteenmile Creek Aqueduct										
144.5	Devil's Alley H/B campsite		●					▲			
149.4	Stickpile Hill H/B campsite		●					▲			
150	Green Ridge State Forest; Lock 60		●	●	●	P	●	▲	●	●	R
152	Rocky Gap State Park	●	●	●	●	P	●	▲	●	●	R
154.1	Sorrel Ridge H/B campsite		●					▲			
155.2	Paw Paw Tunnel: South Entrance-No Bikes										
155.8	Paw Paw Tunnel: North Entrance-No Bikes										
156.2	Paw Paw, WV: Store across the River.	●	●	●	●	P	●		●	●	
157.4	Purslane Run Campground							▲			
162.1	Town Creek H/B campsite		●			P		▲			
162.3	Town Creek Aqueduct										
164.8	Potomac Forks H/B campsite		●					▲			
166.7	Oldtown, MD	●				P	●				
169.2	Pigman's Ferry H/B campsite		●					▲			
173.3	Spring Gap Recreation Area	●	●	●	●	P	●	▲	●		
175.4	Iron's Mountain H/B campsite		●					▲			
175.6	North Branch Locks					P			●		
180.0	Evitt's Creek H/B campsite		●					▲			
180.7	Evitt's Creek Aqueduct										
184.5	Cumberland, MD: Western Trailhead.	●	●	●	●	P		▲	●	●	R
184.5	Western Maryland Scenic Railroad										
184.5	Western Maryland Visitor Center	●	●	●	●	P			●		

● = Food   ● = Water   ● = Telephone   ● = Restrooms   P = Parking
● = Picnic   ▲ = Camping   ● = Boat Ramp   ● = Motel   R = Rentals

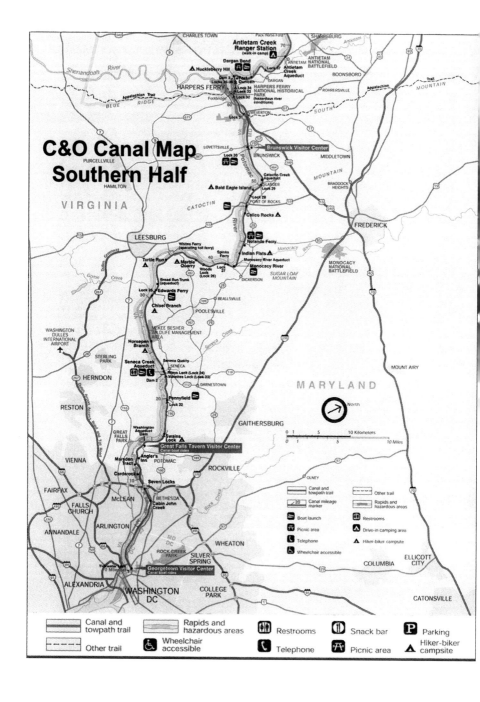

C&O Canal Map
Southern Half

VIRGINIA

MARYLAND

North

| 0 | 1 | 5 | 10 Kilometers |
| 0 | 1 | 5 | 10 Miles |

Canal and towpath trail

Canal mileage marker

Boat launch

Picnic area

Telephone

Wheelchair accessible

Other trail

Rapids and hazardous areas

Restrooms

Drive-in camping area

Hiker-biker campsite

CHARLES TOWN
Pack Horse Ford
SHARPSBURG
Antietam
SHEPHERDSTOWN
Antietam Creek Ranger Station (walk-in camp)
ANTIETAM NATIONAL BATTLEFIELD
Dargan Bend
Lock 37
Antietam Creek Aqueduct
BOONSBORO
Huckleberry Hill
DARGAN
Dam 3
Locks 35-36
Duncan
Lock 34
HARPERS FERRY NATIONAL HISTORICAL PARK (hazardous river conditions)
Lock 33
HARPERS FERRY
Lock 32
Footbridge
ROHRERSVILLE
Appalachian Trail
Shenandoah River
Potomac River
BLUE RIDGE
SOUTH MOUNTAIN
Appalachian Trail
Trail
MOUNTAIN
Lock 31
SILVERTON
LOVETTSVILLE
Lock 30
Brunswick Visitor Center
MIDDLETOWN
PURCELLVILLE
BRUNSWICK
HAMILTON
Catoctin Creek Aqueduct
Lock 29
 LANDER
Bald Eagle Island
Lock 28
POINT OF ROCKS
CATOCTIN MOUNTAIN
BRADDOCK HEIGHTS
FREDERICK
LEESBURG
Catoctin Creek
Calico Rocks
Nolands Ferry
Whites Ferry (operating toll ferry)
Indian Flats
Monocacy River Aqueduct
Monocacy River
MONOCACY NATIONAL BATTLEFIELD
Turtle Run
Marble Quarry
Spinks Ferry
Woods Lock (Lock 26)
SUGAR LOAF MOUNTAIN
DICKERSON
Broad Run Trunk (aqueduct)
Lock 25
Edwards Ferry
BEALLSVILLE
Goose Creek
Chisel Branch
POOLESVILLE
MCKEE BESHER WILDLIFE MANAGEMENT AREA
WASHINGTON DULLES INTERNATIONAL AIRPORT
Horsepen Branch
STERLING PARK
Seneca Creek Aqueduct
Seneca Quarry
SENECA
Rileys Lock (Lock 24)
Violettes Lock (Lock 23)
Dam 2
HERNDON
DARNESTOWN
RESTON
Pennyfield Lock 22
MOUNT AIRY
GAITHERSBURG
Swains Lock
Washington Aqueduct Dam
GREAT FALLS PARK
Great Falls Tavern Visitor Center
Canal boat rides
Anglers Inn
POTOMAC
VIENNA
Marsden Tract
ROCKVILLE
Carderock
OLNEY
Seven Locks
FAIRFAX
FALLS CHURCH
McLEAN
BETHESDA
Cabin John Creek
ANNANDALE
ARLINGTON
WHEATON
ROCK CREEK PARK
COLUMBIA
ELLICOTT CITY
MD DC
SILVER SPRING
Tidewater Lock
Georgetown Visitor Center
Canal boat rides
ALEXANDRIA
WASHINGTON DC
COLLEGE PARK
CATONSVILLE

Canal and towpath trail

Rapids and hazardous areas

Restrooms

Snack bar

Parking

Other trail

Wheelchair accessible

Telephone

Picnic area

Hiker-biker campsite

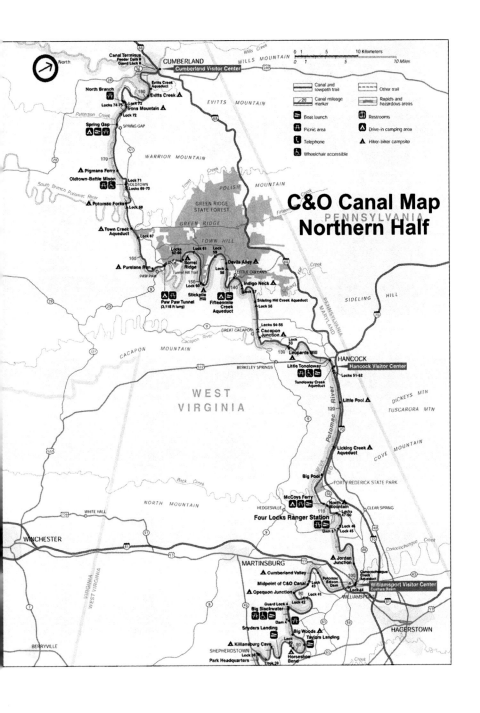

C&O Canal Map
Northern Half

North

CUMBERLAND
Cumberland Visitor Center

Canal and towpath trail
Canal mileage marker
Boat launch
Picnic area
Telephone
Wheelchair accessible

Other trail
Rapids and hazardous areas
Restrooms
Drive-in camping area
Hiker-biker campsite

Canal Terminus
Feeder Dam 8
Guard Lock 8

WILLS MOUNTAIN

Wills Creek

0 1   5   10 Kilometers
0 1   5   10 Miles

North Branch
Evitts Creek Aqueduct
Locks 74-75
Irons Mountain
Lock 72
Spring Gap
SPRING GAP

Evitts Creek

EVITTS MOUNTAIN

WARRIOR MOUNTAIN

Patterson Creek

South Branch Potomac River

Pigmans Ferry
Oldtown-Battle Mixon
OLDTOWN
Lock 71
Locks 69-70
Potomac Forks
Lock 68
Town Creek Aqueduct
Lock 67
Purslane Run

Lock 72

POLISH MOUNTAIN

Town Creek

GREEN RIDGE STATE FOREST

GREEN RIDGE

TOWN HILL

Locks 63-66
Lock 61
Lock 59
Sorrel Ridge
Tunnel Hill Trail
Lock 58
Devils Alley
LITTLE ORLEANS
Indigo Neck
Lock 57
Lock 60
Paw Paw Tunnel (3,118 ft long)
Stickpile Hill
Fifteenmile Creek Aqueduct
Sideling Hill Creek Aqueduct
Lock 56

PENNSYLVANIA
MARYLAND

SIDELING HILL

CACAPON MOUNTAIN

Cacapon River

GREAT CACAPON

Locks 54-55
Cacapon Junction
Lock 53
Leopards Mill
Little Tonoloway
BERKELEY SPRINGS
Tonoloway Creek Aqueduct

HANCOCK
Hancock Visitor Center
Locks 51-52

WEST VIRGINIA

DICKEYS MTN
TUSCARORA MTN

Little Pool

Licking Creek Aqueduct

COVE MOUNTAIN

Back Creek

NORTH MOUNTAIN

Big Pool
FORT FREDERICK STATE PARK

McCoys Ferry
Four Locks Ranger Station
North Mountain
Locks 47-50
Dam 5
Lock 45
CLEAR SPRING

WHITE HALL

WINCHESTER

MARTINSBURG

Jordan Junction

Cumberland Valley
Midpoint of C&O Canal
Lock 43
Opequon Junction
Guard Lock 4
Lock 42
Big Slackwater
Snyders Landing
Dam 4
Killiansburg Cave
SHEPHERDSTOWN
Lock 38
Park Headquarters
Lock 39

Potomac Edison Dam
Conococheague Aqueduct
Williamsport Visitor Center
Cushwa Basin
Lock 44
WILLIAMSPORT

HAGERSTOWN

Big Woods
Taylors Landing
Horseshoe Bend

Conococheague Creek

BERRYVILLE

VIRGINIA
WEST VIRGINIA

Islands
of the Upper Potomac

The islands of the Potomac are covered with trees, which makes them home to many animals and birds. Between Cabin John (mile 8) and the Monocacy River at (mile 42) there are 35 islands. A Wildlife Management Area (WMA) contains 21 of these islands, ranging in size from a few hundred square feet to 243 acres. All of these 21 islands except for one have been designated as a wildlife sanctuary. Numerous songbirds nest and migrate through these islands. During spring and fall migration, large numbers of birds may be seen resting in the trees. On the larger islands, white-tailed deer, wild turkey, beaver, raccoon, and gray and red fox may be seen.

MONTGOMERY COUNTY ISLANDS

High *(Brookmont, m. 5.4)*
Snake *(Little Falls Dam, m. 5.8)*
Sycamore *(Glen Echo, m. 6.7)*
Ruppert *(Glen Echo, m. 6.9)*
Cabin John *(Cabin John, m. 7.5)*
Minnie *(Cabin John, m. 8.2)*
Langley *(Cabin John, m. 8.2)*
Wades *(Cabin John, m. 8.5)*
Swainson *(Lock 10, m. 8.8)*
Plummers *(Am. Legion Br, m. 9.4)*
Vasp *(Carderock, m. 10.0)*
Turkey *(Carderock, m.10.3)*
Herzog *(Carderock, m.10.5)*

Perry *(Carderock, m. 10.7)*
Hermit *(Carderock, m.10.8)*
Offutt *(Carderock, m. 11.1)*
Sherwin *(Great Falls, m. 11.9)*
Bear *(Great Falls, m. 12.7)*
Rocky *(Great Falls, m. 13.8)*
Olmstead *(Great Falls, m. 14.1)*
Conn *(Great Falls, 14.9)*
Bealls *(Potomac, 15.9)*
Gladys *(Potomac, 16.6)*
Clagett *(Tobytown, m. 18.1)*
Watkins *(Tobytown, m. 18.1)*
Grapevine *(Block. Pt., 20.8)*
Katie *(Blockhouse Pt., m. 20.9)*
Elm *(Blockhouse Pt., m 21.3)*
Patowmac *(Block. Pt. m. 21.6)*

Sharpshin *(Seneca, m. 26.0)*
Tenfoot *(McKee-Beshers, 27.0)*
Van Deventer *(McKee-B., m. 28.7)*
Selden *(Poolesville, m. 29.0)*
Harrison *(Poolesville, m. 34.5)*
Mason *(Poolesville, m. 37.3)*

FREDERICK COUNTY ISLANDS

Cox *(Monocacy, m. 42.4)*
Birdsaw *(Noland's Ferry, m. 42.9)*
Meadow *(Noland's Ferry, m. 43.5)*
Noland's *(Noland's Ferry, m. 44.4)*
Heater's *(Point of Rocks, m. 47.4)*
Paton *(Point of Rocks, m. 48.8)*

Mile 0-10   Georgetown and Vicinity

The towpath begins in the Georgetown section of Washington DC at Rock Creek near the end of 29th street Northwest. Rock Creek marks the end of the navigable Potomac River. The canal passes by Georgetown's quaint shops, and through a series of lift locks. Barge rides are available during the summer months.

Starting as a brick walkway, the towpath's gravel/clay surface begins after a few blocks. For the first three miles or so the towpath surface is rough due to the heavy traffic load in this section. An alternative route is the paved Capital Crescent Trail (CCT), which begins at the western end of K Street (under the Whitehurst Freeway), paralleling the C&O. The two trails meet at Fletcher's Boathouse (mile 3.1). In addition to a snack bar, boat and bicycle rentals, and rest rooms are available here. The CCT trail crosses over the towpath about a half mile past Fletcher's Boathouse and turns north to Bethesda and Silver Spring.

Chain bridge to Little Falls Dam (miles 4-6) on the Potomac offers excellent small-mouth bass fishing; Little Falls to Stubblefield Falls offers good catfish and carp, and smallmouth flyfishing. Access to this stretch of the river is very limited, and involves scrambling over rocks.

Lock Seven and Sycamore Island (mile 7) are at Glen Echo, a popular stop for gas, food, and supplies. Since 1971, the National Park Service, at the former Glen Echo Amusement Park, has been offering year-round activities in dance, theater, and the arts. The park also administers an artist-in-residence program providing the public with an opportunity to see artists at work. There are concerts, demonstrations, workshops, and festivals and dances during the warm months.

Between miles 8 and 10 is the area known as seven locks (there are seven liftlocks here). The canal passes under the Capital Beltway at mile 9.3 and you enter the Carderock Recreational Area. Here begins and ends the 1.6-mile Section "C" of the Billy Goat Trail. This lessor-known of the Billy Goat Trails offers a less rigorous trail with opportunity to explore, climb, and fish.

Rewatered Section of the C&O Canal
Miles 0 through 10 are completely rewatered, and offer opportunities for boating, fishing, and watching or photographing aquatic wildlife.

Points of Interest
mile 0.0:   Thompson Boat Center - Bike rentals located two blocks from towpath
mile 1.0:   Capital Crescent Trail
mile 3.1:   Fletcher's Boathouse - Bike and boat rentals; picnic area; parking
mile 4.7:   Maryland State Line
mile 5.8:   Little Falls Pumping Station
mile 7.0:   Glen Echo, Seven Locks, Sycamore Island
mile 8.3:   Lock 8: Boat Ramp
mile 8.6:   Footbridge from Parking; picnic area
mile 9.6:   David Taylor Model Basin - Half mile long building to north
mile 9.9:   Pivot Bridge

River Access / Boat Ramp:
mile 3.1:   Fletcher's Boat House

Locks 1, 2, 3

Mile 0.38 - Below the street level in Georgetown, where the waters from the canal empty into Rock Creek.

The Capital Crescent Trail parallels the towpath for 3 miles.

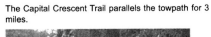

The Georgetown Waterfront and Key Bridge.

Mile 0.5 - Boy Scout Troop 922, from Harve de Grace, Maryland, arrives in Georgetown from their 6-day bike ride from Cumberland, Maryland.

Mile 0.54 - Lock 4.

A plaque reads:

The drop gate on this lift lock was a technological advance over the more common swing gate lock. It was faster and could more easily be operated by a single employee. Only a few drop-gates were installed on the canal, most of them to speed traffic here at Seven Locks where it often took boatmen an hour or more to lock through.

Mile 0.42 - Lock 2 in Georgetown.

Mile 3.13 - Annual spring Shad Run at Fletcher's Boat House.

Fletcher's Boat House, an NPS concession, is a superb fishing and recreational area. The annual Shad Run on the Potomac culminates here with millions of Shad trapped below the Little Falls Dam.

Open from early March through the Fall, Fletcher's rents canoes, boats, and bicycles, and sells bait, tackle and refreshments.

For better handicap accessibility, turn left at the bottom of the access ramp and park on the Canal Road side of the Canal.

Chain Bridge

The suburbs meet the C&O Canal in Montgomery County with several avant-garde spiral bike ramps along the Clara Barton Parkway north of Lock 6. This ramp's path originates at the Sycamore Store on McArthur Boulevard, and leads to the Sycamore Bridge (*next page*).

Mile 5.02 - Lock 5 at Brookmont.

Mile 6.46 - Canoeing at the Montgomery Sycamore Island Club at Glen Echo, just steps from the bridge over the towpath, below.

The footpath from the Clara Barton Parkway parking lot at the spiral bike ramp, to the bridge at Sycamore Island (below). Bottom right, a view of the Canal and towpath from the bridge.

Glen Echo/Seven Locks (mile 7.0) is a popular ice skating destination. Parking can be at a premium, as evidenced by the half-mile long row of cars parked on the edge of the Clara Barton Parkway. Locks 5, 6, 7, and 10 are popular year-round because of nearby roads, shopping, food, and residential neighborhoods.

After parking along the Clara Barton Parkway near Lock 7, a family makes its way to the Canal. Paths and bridges are 1/4 mile to either side of their entrance point. The most popular sites post Park Service "Own Risk" signs.

Mile 8.33 - Lockhouse 8 at Cabin John. Just steps away from nearby neighborhoods, the area is popular year-round.

Mile 8.79 - Lock 10 at Cabin John. Easy, quick access from Interstate 495, or the Clara Barton Parkway makes this the last "close in" access to Washington, DC.

Right: A casual family stroll near Lock 10 just minutes away from their Bethesda home makes for a pleasant break in the day. Frequent access points for the first 9 miles of the C&O Canal make this stretch the most popular.

Mile 9.29 - Lock 12.

At lock 12, any remaining fish stranded in the drying Canal bed desperately congregate in the stagnant waters near the closed lock gate to get oxygen from the dribble of falling water.

Mile 9.37 - Lock 13. This dangerous camera shot was taken from atop the American Legion Bridge.

Mile 10-25   Carderock to Seneca

The towpath here is generally in excellent condition, and the canal basin is still watered. The only exception is around mile 13.5, where a two hundred yard rocky breach requires that you carry your bike. An optional bike detour is available between mile 12.6 and 13.7.

The Carderock Recreational Area provides a range of daytime activities. Parking is usually ample. Large recreational areas for team sports, picnic areas, cooking fire areas, and the Pavilion may be reserved for groups.

Old Angler's Inn is a favorite entry and resting point. The historic Inn has excellent food and drink, and the canal access parking lot across McArthur Blvd. This is also the beginning of the 1.4-mile Section "B" of the Billy Goat Trail.

The major attraction in this section is Great Falls National Park. Canal Boat rides, hiking, climbing, kayaking, a visitor center, and a food concession are just some of the sights and activities and facilities available here. The Billy Goat Trail begins here with a strenuous and rugged 1.7 mile trek around Bear Island.

Passing Great Falls, the towpath becomes much less crowded. Swain's Lock is a pleasant place to stop for a break, snacks, and for bike or canoe rentals. At mile 22.8 are the remains of the Seneca Creek Aqueduct at Riley's Lock, with rentals available at Camp OuterQuest.

Rewatered Section of the C&O Canal

Miles 10 through 22 are completely rewatered, and offer opportunities for boating, fishing, and watching or photographing aquatic wildlife.

Points of Interest

mile 10.9:	Carderock Recreational Area - picnic, rest rooms, water
mile 11.0:	Southern extension entrance to the Billy Goat Hiking Trail; footbridge
mile 12.0:	Marsden Tract; private scout campground
mile 12.6:	Old Angler's Inn
mile 12.6:	Wide Water bicycle detour begins; provides route around rocky breach
mile 13.0:	Southern entrance to Billy Goat Hiking Trail (no bikes)
mile 13.4:	200 yard rocky breach; carry bike
mile 13.7:	Bicycle detour ends
mile 13.8:	Northern entrance to Billy Goat Hiking Trail; Mathers Gorge overlook
mile 14.0:	Foot bridges to Great Falls overlook at Olmstead Island
mile 14.3:	Great Falls Tavern Visitor Center; barge rides are available during the summer
mile 14.3:	Great Falls Snack Bar - Run by Park Service
mile 16.6:	Swain's Lock - snack Bar, bike/canoe rentals, boat ramp
mile 19.6:	Pennyfield Lock - left turn about 100 yards past the Travilah Road; boat ramp
mile 20.1:	Dierssen WMA
mile 21.0:	Blockhouse Point Park - 630 acres; several hiking and equestrian trails
mile 22.1:	Violette's Lock
mile 22.8:	Riley's Lock/Seneca Aqueduct - left turn on Seneca Road from River Road

River Access / Boat Ramp:

mile 22.8:	Seneca Creek/Riley's Lock

Mile 10.41 - Exiting Carderock to the Clara Barton Parkway, the road passes under the C&O Canal and the aqueduct at Carderock.

The Carderock recreational facilities may be reserved for groups of 25-100 from the Park Service. There are three parking lots accessing different area of the Park. The northern parking lot is the terminus for this section of the Billy Goat Trail.

The Billy Goat Trail at Carderock

Mile 10.8 - The Carderock cliffs are great for "learning the ropes." With proper adult supervision, even preteens and children can quickly learn climbing skills. Activities such as this at the C&O Park really bring a family together and reinforce strong personal values and discipline.
Below: a mother double checks the rigging on her children.

Previous page: **Mile 10.8** - The third north-end parking lot at Carderock is the terminus for the Billy Goat Trail, which originates at Great Falls. This hike is a scramble around the rocks and cliffs, just a quarter mile from the parking lot. The tree has a blue trail marker in its center. Carderock Recreation Area is less crowded than Great Falls Park, and there is no entrance fee here.

Mile 11.52 - Footbridge. Because this section of the canal goes through so many neighborhoods and by so many roads, there are many access points making casual walks along the C&O a frequent pastime every season of the year. For safety reasons the bridges are all well-maintained by the Park Service.

Old Angler's Inn

Mile 12.62 - A welcome "oasis" to Canal hikers, the Old Angler's Inn on MacArthur Blvd. is a favorite location to "hike-n-brunch." The Inn is well-known for fine food and atmosphere. C&O parking across the street is access to the Wide Water area. Below is the towpath looking back from Widewater toward Old Angler's access.

A beginners Kayak class returns to Old Angler's Inn for lunch. *Bottom:* Canada Geese break for lunch at Wide Water.

Canal wildlife is abundant in the Wide Water area, a favorite fishing and hiking spot. Although fishing is more productive in the Potomac River just a quarter mile away, the river is a hundred feet lower, after a climb down "serious" rocks and cliffs. A little further on, the towpath becomes impassable by bike. The athletically courageous may attempt to carry their bikes over these rocks.

Jim Emery
Photography

Mile 13.74 - A nearby plaque reads: "Structures such as this stop-lock were designed to divert flood waters from the canal. Wooden planks were dropped into the slots, forming a dam which diverted rushing waters along a stone levee and back into the Potomac."

Mile 13.99 - Lock 15, the first of three at Great Falls, which are the last three of the "Six Locks."

Lock 19

Great Falls

Discovering Miles 10-25

The Billy Goat Trail

This trail starts at a parking lot adjacent to the Old Angler's Inn. Follow the C&O Canal path for perhaps half a mile upstream and take a left onto the marked trail. Two miles of rough up and down follow with good views of the river. The latter half of the trail proceeds along bare cliff-tops not quite as vertical as those on the other side, but having superior views. There are a series of fascinating pot holes caused by erosive of rocks caught in river eddies. Some of these are large enough to stand in.

At the upper end of the trail, the hiker is rewarded with a good view of some of the rocky islands immediately downstream of the falls—some nice shoots and channels frequented by boaters. The trail rejoins the canal towpath near Lock 16. A right takes you back to the parking lot along the canal. To the left, the path climbs up and overlooks the falls.

Trip Distance: simple loop-4 miles. Terrain: rocky with many scrambles. There are several trails, but the most popular winds along the tops of 50 foot cliffs for a mile or two overlooking Mather Gorge, popular playground of whitewater kayakers and rock-climbers.

The Maryland Billygoat Trail is a substantially rougher trail and not as popular as the Virginia Ridge Trail and River Trail across the river, but it offers some good scrambling over rocks and some nice woods. The C&O Canal with its walking/biking path passes through the area and a number of more recent locks in better condition can be viewed.

The Falls themselves are spectacular. This is a seething mass of Class VI+ whitewater and masses of rock. Rather than one large waterfall a la Niagra, this is a 50 foot drop in the river interrupted by a chaos of rocky spires and basins. There are as many ways of running the falls as there are ways of dying in the process. Indeed, people have died in these rapids. Despite the signs, boaters and hikers alike have caught the wrong end of Mother Nature. Just down stream (on the tops of the 50-foot cliffs) there is a picnic area.

Great Falls of the Potomac
Charles Danforth / danforth@pha.jhu.edu

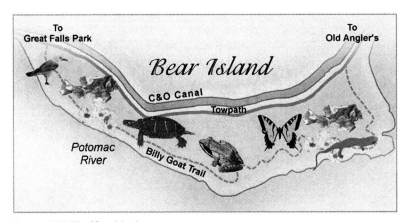

Plants and Wildlife of Bear Island
The prothonotary warbler is a strikingly beautiful bird known for its delicate "sweet-sweet-sweet" chirp.
Virginia bluebells grow in large patches scattered throughout Bear Island's rich woods and bloom in spring.
Painted turtles can be seen in shallow ponds.
The wood frog, with its hoarse clacking croak, prefers rich moist woods for its habitat.
The tiger swallowtail butterfly is one of six types of swallowtails on the island.
Carolina tassel-rue, a western Maryland species, was carried to Bear Island by floodwaters of the

Bear Island and the Potomac Gorge

The Potomac River's Potomac Gorge is a group of ecosystems unique to this part of the river. Species from different places and altitudes have been brought together by the geology of the river basin, and the advent of periodic flooding by the river. More than 50 of Maryland's rare, threatened or endangered plant and animal species exist within the Gorge. The Potomac Gorge has one of the highest concentrations of globally rare natural environments in the nation, including twelve globally-rare plant species and four animal species.

At higher elevations on the island, floodwaters deposit soil that supports diverse forests and native spring wildflowers. Throughout Bear island, periodic flooding has created ponds that serve as breeding grounds for amphibians such as frogs and salamanders. Along the lower elevations, flooding strips away soils, leaving behind sand and gravel or bare rock, creating prairie and savanna habitats. These environments support many rare and unusual plants. These plants are quick to adapt to changing land conditions caused by river flooding, where most other species may find the environment too hostile.

Bear Island's Billy Goat Trail explores these unusual habitats and their rare plant and animal species, and provides a rare glimpse at the ecology along the Potomac Gorge. The Potomac Gorge is the East Coast's largest and most pristine example of a "fall line" landscape—a series of river rapids that mark the change from the hard, ancient bedrock of the Piedmont plateau to the soft, sandy deposits of the coastal plain. The rocky outcrops along the Billy Goat Trail are typical of a fall line. It is this geology that has brought together this unusual mix of plants and animals on Bear Island.

Olmstead Island

A boardwalk across a fragile ecosystem ends at two spectator decks overlooking the falls. Pick up the boardwalk (accessible to strollers and wheelchairs) between Locks 17 and 18.

Many of the plants alongside and under the protective boardwalk are Threatened and Endangered Species. Footsteps in this fragile ecosystem could cause irreparable harm to these delicate life-forms living under relatively hostile environmental conditions. The still canal waters, land, and rocks are teeming with reptiles, amphibians, mammals, birds, plants, and of course, insects.

Mile 14.05 - There's a bridge and a boardwalk across Olmstead island, accessible only by foot. Here's the view (right) from the top of that bridge.

Mile 14.3 - This former tavern is now a museum of the C & O Canal. There's a gift shop, displays of canal works, movies and a bookstore. It is located at Lock 20. Nearby is the access to Olmstead Island and the Billy Goat Trail.

Mile 13.85 - Nearby is the trail head for the Billy Goat trail, which is a vigorous scramble over all these rocks.

Great Falls Trails Map

Short trails are marked with yellow signs
More lengthy and challenging trails are marked with blue signs

Great Falls Park has 15 miles of trails for hiking and exploring. A park trail map and a self guiding brochure for the Potomac Canal Trail are available at the visitor center. Five miles of multiple use trails provide opportunity for horseback riding and bicycling.

Most of the trails are fast, smooth, wide single-tracks or doubletracks with a few climbs. Some of the best views of the big drops at Great Falls can be viewed from the Olmstead Island trails.

The Trails at Great Falls

Short trails are marked with yellow signs. More challenging trails are marked with blue signs.

Lock 16 Spur Trail (0.3 mile) This trail is quite short and accessible.

Lock 19 Loop Trail (0.5 mile) A very short and easy trail, it begins at the Gold Mine Loop and ends at Lock 19.

Angler's Spur Trail (0.5 mile) This trail is uphill and leads through as thick wooded area. It begins at the Angler's Inn.

Woodland Trail (0.6 mile) The Woodland Trail is quite easy to traverse for beginners. It begins at Gold Mine loop and passes through old, overgrown 1860's-era earthworks.

Berma Road Trail (3.3 miles) An easy one+ mile level hike. This Trail runs along Lock 16 and ends at Angler's Inn.

How the C&O Canal Really Began

George Washington's plan to make the Potomac River navigable as far as the Ohio River Valley began with the construction of the Patowmack Canal. This was the shortest route between tidewater, with access to East Coast and trans-Atlantic trade, and the Ohio River, with access to the western frontier. Political obstacles had to be overcome. This venture, first proposed in 1785 was formally initiated in 1803.

The Potomac presented many physical obstacles to travel. To make the river navigable by shallow draft boats, the Patowmack Company had to dredge portions of the riverbed and skirt five areas of falls. By far the most demanding task was the successful building a canal with locks to bypass the Great Falls of the Potomac.

Thousands of boats locked through at Great Falls, carrying flour, whiskey, tobacco, and iron downstream; carrying cloth, hardware, firearms, and other manufactured products upstream. Vessels varied from crudely constructed rafts to the long narrow keelboat that could carry up to 20 tons of cargo. The trip took 3 to 5 days down to Georgetown and 10 to 12 days poling against the current back to Cumberland.

High construction costs and insufficient revenues bankrupted the company. Extremes of high and low water restricted use of the canal to only a month or two each year. The tolls collected could not even pay interest on the company debt. The Patowmack Company succumbed in 1828, turning over its assets and liabilities to the Chesapeake and Ohio Canal Company. The new company abandoned the Patowmack Canal in 1830 for an even more ambitious undertaking: a man-made waterway stretching from Georgetown to Cumberland on the Maryland side of the river.

the
Patowmack
Canal
of the
Great Falls,
Virginia

The Patowmack Canal Interpretive Trail is accessible by wheelchair as far as Lock 1. The trail surface consists of compacted soil with no curbs.

The Trails at Great Falls Park, Virginia

Great Falls Park, Virginia is 800 acres in size and has 15 miles of trails, 5 of which are multiple use trails to include opportunities for mountain biking and horseback riding. The trail system offers a wide variety of environments for exploration. The river trail follows the Potomac river from the falls overlooks downstream along the scenic Mather Gorge; the Patowmack Canal trail follows the ruins of this historic canal and the ruins of the canal town of Matildaville; the Old Carriage Road trail, the Ridge trail and Mine Run trail follow upland oak forests; the swamp trail follows along a unique swamp habitat and lowland forest. You may connect several trails in loops with distances varying from 1 mile to 4 miles.

Other Great Falls Park Trails

Patowmack Canal Trail
Swamp Trail
Difficult Run Trail
Matildaville Trail
Mine Run Trail
Trails to Riverbend Park

The River Trail

The River Trail begins downstream of the Visitor Center and falls overlooks, following the narrow Mather Gorge, named after the first director of the National Park Service, Stephen Mather. The trail is well established and crosses very rocky terrain along 30 to 70 foot cliffs and offers spectacular views of the gorge and the shoreline of the Potomac River. The trail is easy to follow by the blue blazes marked on the trees. The River Trail extends 1.5 miles downstream to Cowhoof Rock where it then meets with the Ridge Trail. From that point one can choose to return via the Ridge Trail or continue another half mile downstream to Difficult Run, the southern border of the park. Several loops have shorter distances, ranging from a half mile loop to a 4 mile loop. A popular hike takes you down the River Trail 1/2 mile and returns along the historic Patowmack Canal Trail for a 1 mile loop.

Old Carriage Road

An out-and-back trail. Great for beginners, this trail is mainly flat and leads to another trail, the Ridge Trail. (3.2 miles.)

Ridge Trail

A little more challenging, the Ridge Trail offers greater inclines and hills to tackle as well as some roots to jump. While a little challenging at times, this is still a "beginners" trail. The wonderful scenic views along the river make this trip a "must see" when in the area. (3 miles round-trip.)

Great Falls of the Po-

Swain's Lock

Mile 16.64 - Swain's Lock.
Open 7 Days a week, 10
a.m. to 6 p.m.
Directions: Exit 49 off
Capital Beltway, west
on River Road toward
Potomac. Two miles past
Potomac Village, left on
Swains Lock Road, to
end.

Swain's Lock is a favorite C&O Canal access point. The Swain's Lock area offers Montgomery County residents convenient canal access, and well-maintained park facilities. The refreshment stand offers snacks and drinks. Bike and Canoe rentals are available.

Mile 19.63 - Pennyfield Lock at Potomac in early Spring. Below right: Montgomery County's Muddy Branch Creek meets Pennyfield Lock, and flows under the C&O Canal before emptying into the Potomac River.

Dierssen Wildlife Management Area (WMA)

This marshy, 40-acre tract of land, one-half mile west of Pennyfield Lock, between the C&O Canal and the Potomac River was donated to the state for use as a waterfowl sanctuary. Two man-made ponds, as well as adjacent forest make for a quiet interlude for strollers on the Canal towpath. Trails wind around one of the impoundments, to the Potomac River.

Mile 20 - The area between the canal and the Potomac is usually narrow, but Dierssen WMA is full of ponds and attracts waterfowl. This and the adjacent 630 acre Blockhouse Point Conservation Park have 25 species of fish, 8 species of amphibians, 7 species of reptiles, 39 species of nesting birds, and 14 species of mammals found within its unmarked boundaries.

Mile 22.12 - Lock 23 or Violette's Lock. On the right is the lock, on the left is Inlet Lock #2. The inlet lock was a feeder to keep the canal watered but it also served as an entry point. There's a footbridge over the lock and the inlet lock above, which two canoeists are using to carry their canoe to the Potomac River.

The National Park Service does a good job of keeping the posted picnic areas in the park well-maintained. However, their "cookie-cutter" approach does not leave any room for individuality or style. The picture of the picnic area, at right, could be of almost any other lock. Tranquil, clean, and pleasantly beautiful.

Violette's Lock, viewed from the towpath side.

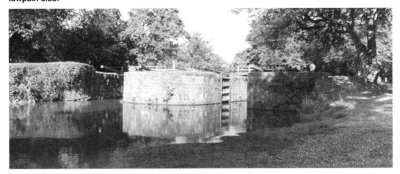

Seneca Creek

Mile 22.82 - Seneca, Maryland at Riley's Lock. Seneca Creek winds through Montgomery County and empties into the Potomac here. The aqueduct originally had three arches; the repaired remains of the third can be seen below on the right.

Maryland Department of Natural Resources (DNR) Fisheries Restoration and Enhancement Programs stocked 1,750 rainbow trouts in the year 2000, and 5,500 in 2001. An additional 5,750 rainbows were stocked in Seneca Creek in the spring of 2002. Almost 430,000 rainbows were stocked in nearly 100 Maryland streams, ponds, and lakes in the spring of 2002.

Mile 22.88 - Tscheffeley. You can reach the mill by a path that starts shortly after the aqueduct and runs on the opposite side of the canal. The canal opens up to a basin just as the path starts. This is the bottom of the mill race. Water was diverted from Seneca Creek and ran through this race to power the mill.

On the first warm day of spring, joggers and walkers enjoy the towpath at Seneca/Riley's Lock. This is the last major access point to the C&O Canal and Potomac River for the Washington DC metro area suburbs. While food, water, and public restrooms are available here, it can take more than a little reconnaissance and question-asking to find these facilities.

Mile 23 - Riley's Lock Picnic Area in late April.

Mile 25-40   Seneca to Dickerson

Passing Riley's Lock and Seneca Creek Aqueduct, the conditions change radically. The canal bed is not watered and has been reclaimed by overgrowth. The wide towpath has become a dual track path.

The first of the hiker-biker campsites is located in this section. Each site contains a water pump and Jiffy John. Campsites are occupied on a first-come, first-serve basis. A word of caution: the water from campsite pumps should be boiled just to be safe. Groundwater conditions vary from site to site, and even from season to season.

McKee-Beshers Wildlife Management Area at mile 27.2 is a natural flood plain, with several trails crossing the forest, traversing Beaver ponds. Maryland birding clubs have noted over 200 species of birds within the area boundaries.

The major point of interest in this section is White's Ferry, the only working ferry on the Potomac. The ferry is used daily by commuters to cross over to Leesburg, VA ($1 for bikes, $3 for cars) and where lodging and stores are available. White's Ferry is a popular destination/starting point for hikers and bikers. A hot-food snack bar makes this a "must" stop for Canal goers. With a large picnic area and numerous tables, and bike and canoe rentals, private and corporate groups are encouraged to spend an afternoon here. Good Crappie and smallmouth fishing are found on the river, especially in spring and fall.

Dickerson Conservation Area provides C&O Canal parking and access. There is usually water in this section of the canal, although some sections may be blocked with access and maintenance landfill paths across the canal. The adjacent Dickerson PEPCO generating station is within a mile's walk, making this is a popular access point for winter fisherman.

Points of Interest

mile 26.1: Horsepen Branch campsite
mile 27.2: McKee-Beshers Wildlife Management Area. Footbridge to Maddux Island
mile 30.5: Chisel Branch campsite (located near the Edward's Ferry access point)
mile 30.8: Edward's Ferry - From Poolesville, take Whites Ferry Road west for about 1 mile. Turn left on Edward's Ferry Road. Follow to end (about 4.5 miles)
mile 30.8: Edward's Ferry lock and boat ramp
mile 30.8: Jarboe's Store
mile 31.9: Broad Run Trunk Aqueduct ruins and campsite
mile 34.5: Turtle Run campsite
mile 35.5: White's Ferry-snack bar; camping
mile 35.5: White's Ferry-From Poolesville, take Whites Ferry Road west for about 6 m
mile 35.5: Norris House Inn, Leesburg, 800-644-1806
mile 35.5: Best Western, Leesburg, 703-777-9400
mile 38.1: Marble Quarry campsite
mile 39.4: Wood's Lock
mile 39.6: Dickerson Regional Park; footbridge leads to a fishing area

River Access / Boat Ramp:

Edward's Ferry, m. 30.8; White's Ferry, m. 35.3

Hugh's Hollow and McKee-Beshers WMA

Mile 27.2 - A juvenile black crowned night heron at McKee-Beshers WMA.

Above: Barrel Owl. Left: A young Blue Heron stalks the

The McKee-Beshers Wildlife Management Area (WMA) is mostly a flood plane of the Potomac River. Within it are some farmed fields and aquatic ponds. The flat and mostly open land has some dirt roads that are good for running. Hikers will find trails for miles and miles, meandering through the forests, fields and wetlands. The C&O Canal and towpath border the area. Hunters enjoy the pursuit of white-tailed deer, woodcock, squirrels, waterfowl, and many other species.

What To See

McKee-Beshers WMA has an active beaver population which is always busy damming streams to create ponds. Biologists deliberately flood forests during the fall and winter in "greentree reservoirs." These attract the colorful wood ducks as well as other waterfowl which migrate through or spend the winter here. More than 200 species of birds have been documented over the years by local bird clubs. Birds with special needs for forests or fields find sanctuary here.

What To Do

Hikers will find trails for miles meandering through the forests, fields and wetlands. The C&O Canal and trail border the area. Hunters enjoy the pursuit of white-tailed deer, woodcock, squirrels, waterfowl and many other species. McKee-Beshers WMA offers special designated areas for training hunting dogs. Field trials, where dogs and humans match their skills with nature, are also held here in the spring and fall.

From the Capital Beltway, take Exit 39 (River Road) west toward Potomac. Proceed for approximately 11 miles to the intersection of River Road and MD 112, Seneca Road. Turn left and continue for about 2 1/2 miles. McKee-Beshers is on your left as go west on River Road.

From Riley's Lock, follow the towpath northwest. Three miles up, just past mile post 26, is Horsepen Branch Campground. At the water pump (this water should be treated before drinking), a trail to the right passes over the dry Canal bed into the WMA. For additional information, contact the Gwynnbrook Work Center at (410) 356-9272.

Mile 27.2 - McKee-Beshers Wildlife Management Area at the Potomac River. This important wildlife refuge area is know by area birding clubs to be the home of or the migratory route of over 200 species of birds. Wild Turkeys and Beaver are common, as are deer.

Mile 30.5 - Chisel Branch is the name of a nearby stream; this campsite is fairly close to the canal.

Mile 30.84 - Edward's Ferry. Many neighboring properties follow prescribed safe deer management and hunting policies, assuring conservation of both the animals and the land that they feed on.

The QDMA promotes: safe hunting practices; adequate harvests of adult does; restraint of harvesting young bucks; education, cooperation, and involvement with biologists and law enforcement.

Mile 30.84 - Edward's Ferry boatramp.

Lock 25, Edward's Ferry Lockhouse.

Mile 30.84 - Jarboe's store at Edward's Ferry closed in 1906. It was run by former locktenders John Walters and Charlie Poole.

Mile 31.9 - This was a wooden aqueduct for Broad Run Trunk. The footpath/bridge you see follows the canal. Parallel to that is the aqueduct, with the wooden part missing. In the front is Broad Run.

Mile 35.5 - The canal at White's Ferry.

White's Ferry is the last operating ferry across the Potomac River, and the only operating cable-guided (captive) fresh water ferry along the East Coast. The ferry connects scenic areas of Montgomery County, Maryland and Loudoun County, Virginia. A ferry has operated at this river crossing for over 150 years.

For a romantic getaway, a family outing, or a group function, the site has picnic tables overlooking the historic Potomac River. Pack your own provisions, or, better yet, pick up provisions from the White's Ferry Store and Snack Bar for a picnic to remember. The store has rowboats and canoes for rent as well as groceries and bait. The site is a popular choice for company picnics and family reunions.

White's Ferry is a popular location for fishing, especially for smallmouth bass. The Maryland Department of Natural Resources classifies the area from Seneca to the Mouth of the Monocacy River as "catch-and-release" for bass. Novice and experienced fishermen alike enjoy the catch at White's Ferry. Bass, Carp, Catfish, Crappie and Perch are among the plentiful fish of the Potomac. Live bait is available, as are fishing tackle and supplies, right at the White's Ferry Store and Snack Bar.

Mile 35.5 - White's Ferry and Store.

White's Ferry

Mile 39.6 - Dickerson Conservation Area and the adjoining Pepco power plant provide large undisturbed forest areas essential to migratory birds.

Mile 40-50   Dickerson to Lander Lock

During winter, the Dickerson Power Plant is a major fishing destination. The power plant discharge into the river warms the water to 50-55 degrees directly below the plant, and warms the waters on the Maryland side for four miles downriver to White's Ferry. These warmer waters make the fish more active, and therefore more active feeders. Fishing in the discharge channel is usually productive for smallmouth bass, and sometimes crappie.

A White Water Kayak and Olympic Training Course has been developed in the discharge channel at the power plant, by the Center of Excellence (BCE) and the Canoe Cruisers Assoc.

This section of the Canal contains the beautiful, "endangered" Monocacy Aqueduct, a 500 foot, seven arch, stone bridge used to carry the canal over the Monocacy River. In the 1970's the Park service erected temporary skeleton around the aqueduct to shore up damage caused by repeated flooding. Nearly thirty years later the supports remain in place.

At Heater's Island, migrating waterfowl include mallards, wood ducks, black ducks, mergansers, gadwall and Canada geese. Wild turkeys thrive, and songbirds nest here in the spring and summer. Anglers will find plenty of bass, bluegill, sunfish, carp, eel, and catfish.

Trail and Canal conditions are traditionally poor in the mile or two prior to Point of Rocks; lots mud holes can be expected during wet months. The rest of the towpath is in good shape.

Access to the Canal from the town of Point of Rocks is by way of a wooden one-lane bridge over the canal bed. Ample parking is provided. There are two stores/deli's about a block off the towpath, making the town a necessary food and supply stop for Canal hikers and campers.

After the C&O Canal failed in 1924, the railroad built a second railroad track in the abandoned canal bed; however, the towpath is still intact. The Canal towpath temporarily follows a paved driveway past a small home. The unpaved towpath resumes just west of the Route 15 Bridge, the main highway from Frederick, Maryland to Leesburg, Virginia.

Points of Interest

mile 41.0: Dickerson Pepco Power Plant
mile 41.5: Spinks Ferry
mile 42.1: Monocacy Aqueduct
mile 42.2: Footbridge over Canal
mile 42.8: Monocacy Nat. Res. Area - 1,800 acres hunting, fishing, hiking and horse-back riding
mile 42.8: Monocacy Aqueduct
mile 42.4: Indian Flats campsite
mile 44.4: Noland's Ferry and Picnic Area
mile 47.6: Camp Kanawha; private camping
mile 47.6: Calico Rocks campsite
mile 48.0: Heater's Island WMA - Accessible by boat. Excellent Winter Waterfowl hunting
mile 48.2: Point of Rocks, MD - Route 15 bridge overhead; food; camping

River Access / Boat Ramp:

mile 42.1: Monocacy
mile 44.4: Noland's Ferry
mile 48.2: Point of Rocks

Mile 41.46 - Also known as Spink's Ferry, this was the target of a Confederate attack during the Civil War. General Hill of the Confederate army was to destroy the Monocacy Aqueduct but Thomas Walter, the Lock 27 lock keeper, persuaded him to drain the canal at Lock 27 instead. General Hill agreed, particularly because he didn't have the supplies to destroy the aqueduct. He drilled the masonry and placed a charge and did manage enough damage to disrupt service. The lock keeper was nearly discharged after the incident for collaborating with the Confederates, but the locals were impressed by his efforts to save the aqueduct and supported him enough to allow him to keep his job.

Mile 42.19 - At 516 feet and with 7 arches, the Monocacy Aqueduct is the longest of all 11 of the canal's aqueducts. It is currently supported with the aid of steel beams (flood damage), but a restoration project has been announced by the park service.

June, 1998:

Monocacy Aqueduct on Endangered List

Dickerson MD— First Lady Hillary Rodham Clinton toured the Monocacy Aqueduct and helped announce that the aqueduct is one of the nation's 11 Most Endangered Historic Places.

"We cannot save historical sites if people don't know they exist," Mrs. Clinton said, urging park enthusiasts who attended the announcement to spread the word about the aqueduct and other endangered sites.

Mrs. Clinton said her husband's administration is committed to the Save The Treasures Millennium Program, which included a proposed $50 million for preservation.

Noland's Ferry

Mile 47.65 - Calico Rocks is fairly typical of the canal campsites. There's a fire ring, picnic table, and lots of space to pitch your tent. Up by the path, there's a water pump and port-a-john. Caution: it is advisable to boil water from the campsite water pumps before drinking. Groundwater conditions vary from site to site and season to season.

Mile 47.79 - The railroad station at Point of Rocks hosts the MARC commuter train, from Martinsburg WV to Washington, DC. Stop by on a weekday evening and you'll see a host of people in business attire leaving the train.

Mile 47 - The waterfront sold to the Frederick County Fish and Game Protective Association is now known as Camp Kanawha. Kanawha is the name of the Indian tribe that had a palisade on a nearby island.

Mile 48.40 - This 788' right-of-way was one of the most hotly contested between the canal and the railroad.

Mile 48.2 - The original bridge pivoted to allow clearance for passing boats. Though not in use today, the bridge is access from the town of Point of Rocks to the parking lot and to fishing along the Potomac River. It's only a single lane and doesn't look that sturdy, but it's safe to drive over.

Mile 48.93 - a view of the Potomac River from the Point of Rocks boat ramp. Overhead (out of view) is the Route 15 bridge from Frederick County, MD to Loudoun County, VA. Centered in the picture is Sugarloaf Mountain, about five miles away at the county line of Frederick and Montgomery.

Mile 50-60   Lander Lock to Harpers Ferry

Lander Lock at mile 50.9 is the only significant Canal access between Point of Rocks and Brunswick. It is a frequent fishing and hiking spot for locals wanting to avoid the crowds and tourists. The lock house is in very good shape. The last locktender lived here until 1962 and the Park Service still uses it as a contact station. If you continue over the lock bridge, there is additional parking, and it will take you down to a fishing area on the Potomac. The towpath to the left leads to Bald Eagle Island Campground, an unassuming camping site.

Mile 51.5 is the site of the Catoctin Creek Aqueduct. This aqueduct completely collapsed several years ago and has since been replaced by a footbridge. A few miles past, you enter the Brunswick, Maryland area. There is an RV campground along the river. The towpath is quite bumpy here, as traffic uses it to access the a campground. Route 17/287 crosses the Potomac here at mile 55. This road runs south to Purcellville, VA, where you can catch the western terminus of the W&OD Trail.

Brunswick is situated in the southwestern edge of Frederick County Maryland. It is six miles east of Harpers Ferry, on the southwest side of the Catoctin Mountain. The town has several parks, fishing and boating on the Potomac River, the C&O Canal towpath, and a museum with one of the largest model train layouts on the east coast. The Veteran's Day Parade and Brunswick Railroad Days, held in November, are the city's two largest events.

An old airfield has become two hundred camp sites at the Brunswick Family Campground. The large, forested campground provides a boatramp to the river. There is a required permit and charge which may be obtained from the Brunswick town hall or, in season, from the campground.

In May, the Brunswick, MD (Frederick County) Family Campground is the site for Potomac River Awareness Day, a family event, including canoeing, kayaking, fishing and water rescue demonstrations, a river cleanup, triathlon and other activities.

At mile 58, a red brick lock house—the Casper W. Weaver House—marks the point where the Appalachian Trail (AT) joins the towpath. The Weaver House is a historic landmark held by the Park Service, and is not open to the public.

The Appalachian Trail is a 2,167-mile hiking trail that runs from Maine to Georgia across the top of the Appalachian Mountain Chain. After making the short hop across Maryland, the trail comes down off the ridge for a three mile stretch along the C&O Canal. At mile 61, the AT crosses the Potomac River into West Virginia at Harpers Ferry.

Points of Interest

mile 50.3:   Bald Eagle Island campsite
mile 50.9:   Lander Lock 29
mile 51.5:   Catoctin Creek Aqueduct (Ruins)
mile 54.0:   Brunswick, MD; recreation area
mile 58.0:   Appalachian Trail joins towpath
mile 58.0:   Weverton; the Casper W. Weaver House

River Access / Boat Ramp:
mile 54.0:   Brunswick

Mile 50.7 - Between Lander Lock and Bald Eagle Island Campground.

The towpath at left is maintained in good condition here, as a hard-pack maintenance road for the National Park Service. Lander Lock, Lock 29, is a main access point for National Park Service maintenance vehicles in this section, with a locked gate across the towpath. This is also a frequent Canal entry point for local hikers, bikers and fishermen.

The canal, by name only in this area, is a tree-filled gully with occasional swampy sections (left side of picture). Outhouses and water are available at most of the Hiker/ Biker campsites.

The rail road, with its right-of-way, has encroached into the old canal in many areas with the gravel embankment of the tracks filling half of the width of the old canal. The sight of this can be both disheartening and disturbing. If the railroad had its way, there would have been no canal.

Mile 50.3 - Bald Eagle Island Campground. A picnic table, campfire site, and a view of the river. A basic campsite.

Mile 51.53 - This picture is a combination of three elements. The first is the single remaining arch of the Catoctin Creek Aqueduct, on the right. The missing two arches collapsed in 1973. Behind it you can see an arch of the B & O railroad bridge. On top of them both is the steel and wood foot bridge the National Park Service built after the collapse. It is built right beside the remains of the aqueduct.

Mile 52.51 - Little Catoctin Creek Culvert.

Mile 54 - An old airfield was made into two hundred camp sites, where you are likely to find a lot of trailers. There is a charge, and you need to get a permit from the Brunswick town hall or, in season, from the campground.
Below: The boat ramp opens to a good part of the Potomac.

Mile 54-55 - Brunswick, Maryland. Boy Scout Troop 1970 of Reston VA, enjoyed a day on the C&O Canal and took these photographs which show that the magnificent river vistas are worth the trip here.

Appalachian National Scenic Trail

The Appalachian Trail crosses the Potomac toward Maryland at Harpers Ferry on the Goodloe Byron Memorial Bridge.

Mile 58 - Weverton, Lock 31. Casper W. Weaver attempted to establish an industrial area much like the one at Harpers Ferry. His high rents failed to attract enough business and the town ultimately failed.

The Weverton Trail is a side route off of the Appalachian Trail. It begins with a steep incline up the hill following the Appalachian Trail. The Weverton Cliffs trail branches from the main trail to a very scenic view overlooking the Potomac River.

Mile 60-70   Harpers Ferry to Antietam Creek

This is a favorite section of the canal. The major points of interest in this section are Harpers Ferry and Antietam Aqueduct. Both locations played a major roles in Civil War history. This is where John Brown attempted to inspire the local slaves to rebel. The John Brown abolitionist revolt at the Harpers Ferry Arsenal was one of the major events leading to the Civil War. Several years later, at Antietam Creek just outside Sharpsburg, MD, the Union and Confederate armies fought the bloodiest battle of the war.

This section is about an hour's drive from Washington or Baltimore. The towpath here is well maintained. Fishing the Potomac River and the confluence of the Shenandoah River is a prime attraction for Harpers Ferry Park visitors. Exploring the Harpers Ferry town shops can make for a fun afternoon in itself. There are riverside colonial ruins, and numerous trails to explore. Ranger-guided tours are offered in the park from May 27-June 30, and special park events and concerts are held year-round. Whitewater rafting is popular here (see Outfitters and Guides, on page 161). Call 304-535-6298 for more information about park activities.

Maryland Heights has a number of fine hiking trails, and is a favorite rock climbing area with predominantly intermediate-level rock faces. The rock climbing here is by permit only, after a qualifying checkout of gear, skills, and knowledge. This is not the place to learn rock climbing. It can be challenging for both the intermediate and the advanced climber. There are, however, a few climbs that beginners can make with proper equipment and a licensed guide.

The Antietam Creek Aqueduct is one of the best preserved aqueducts on the C&O Canal. Although no longer watered, the aqueduct looks as if it could still carry barges under it. Today, park maintenance vehicles are still able to cross the aqueduct. Antietam Creek Recreation Area provides camping ($10 per night), restrooms, and parking.

Maryland DNR Fisheries Restoration and Enhancement Programs stocked 5,000 rainbow trout in Antietam Creek, and 7,500 rainbow trout in Fifteenmile Creek in the spring of 2002.

Points of Interest

mile 60.2: Harpers Ferry—about 1 mile north at top of hill
mile 60.2: Sandy Hook
mile 60.7: Footbridge to Harpers Ferry, WV (AMTRAK Station)
mile 60.7: Harpers Ferry—snack bars are near the railroad station; there is a restaurant at Hilltop House
mile 60.7: Maryland Heights
mile 61.3: Footbridge across canal; hiking trail to top of Maryland Heights
mile 62.9: Huckleberry Hill campsite
mile 64.9: Dargan Bend Recreation Area and boat ramp
mile 67.0: Mountain Lock and Recreation Area
mile 69.3: Antietam Aqueduct
mile 69.4: Antietam Creek Recreation Area ($10 Fee/Night)
mile 69.4: Burnside Bridge; Antietam Campground; water

River Access / Boat Ramp:

Dargan bend, m. 64.9; Mountain Lock Recreational Area, m. 67; Antietam Creek Recreational Area, m. 69.4.

Harpers Ferry, WVa

The town of Harpers Ferry is situated at the junction of the Potomac and Shenandoah Rivers where Maryland, Virginia, and West Virginia meet. It is best known for the site of John Brown's raid in 1859. Three different presentations are available at the John Brown Museum. Reservations are required for a guided tour by the park ranger and for a self-guided tour. Reservations must be made in writing at least three weeks in advance. Numerous museums, exhibits and trails explore the history of Harpers Ferry. You can visit the nearby Kennedy House, or shop the quaint shops in this beautiful little town, or rock climb nearby Maryland Heights.

Mile 60.2 - left: Harpers Ferry town. Boy Scout Troop 922, from Havre de Grace, Maryland, visited here on their bike trip from Cumberland to Georgetown. Above: a good view of the towpath through Harpers Ferry, taken from the Railroad tunnel.

Left: John Brown's Fort, Harpers Ferry. Below: Jefferson Rock.

Right: The C & O Bicycle Patrol.
They're volunteers who ride
around looking for trouble or
offering assistance.

Mile 60.23 - Sandy Hook. The point at which the Shenandoah River empties into the Potomac. The next few locks are close together, because of the relatively quick change in elevation. There are some locks on the Shenandoah River and throughout Harpers Ferry.

Maryland Heights Trail Information

Discover ruins of old Civil War forts and campsites and catch the spectacular views. From The Point in Lower Town (where the Potomac and Shenandoah rivers meet) to the Overlook Cliffs it is a 4.2 miles (about 3 hours) round-trip. From The Point to the Stone Fort it is 6 miles (about 4 hours) round-trip. The Combined Trail is marked with green blazes; the Overlook Cliff Trail is marked with red blazes; the Stone Fort Trail is marked with blue blazes.

There is no water supply and there are no restrooms on Maryland Heights. The trails include some strenuous uphill sections.

Maryland Heights, across from Harpers Ferry

Maryland Heights Rock Climbing

Rock climbing is allowed on the cliff face of Maryland Heights by permit only. Special regulations regarding rock climbing as well as permits may be obtained at the Ranger Station or Information Center in the Lower Town. Registrants must possess and use approved climbing equipment. A check-out is required.

The area of Harpers Ferry is close enough for day trips. It's about the closest spot for over 300 feet lead climbs. Park in Harpers Ferry and walk on the tourist bridge across the river. A favorite is "Hard Up," a 5.7 climb that goes up a crack in the left side of the old sign. (It's huge) There are also numerous 5.0-5.4 climbs here on the right side of the face. You can rappel down the large corner. In town there is also Jefferson Rock, which has a dead horizontal 10 foot crack. It was the first 5.12 in the area.

There are 26 named climbs at Maryland Heights, with 5.1 to 5.11 difficulty ratings, making these rocks challenging for beginners and novices, and can be challenging for advanced climbers. With the guidance of licensed trainers, there are easy climbs for beginners and novices.

Mile 60.7 - Lock 33, opposite Harpers Ferry. This area was severely damaged in the flood of January 1996.

Mile 62.44 - There are two locks within a tenth of a mile of each other. There's not much left except the canal and that little brown sign NPS put up that says "Lock 36." The lockhouse was shared with the dam 3 inlet lock.

Mile 62.33 - Nestled away in the woods is the lockhouse for the inlet lock and lock 36.

Inside the lockhouse, two fireplaces share a single chimney and dominate the structure. The start of the basement is marked where the red bricks give way to a stone foundation.

Mile 62.9 - The picnic table is close to the river. Huckleberry Hill is one of the smaller sites. But, like all of the C&O Canal campsites, it is clean and well-maintained.

Mile 64.89 - There's a boat launch as well as parking and picnic tables but no camping at Dargan Bend

Limestone kilns, used until about 1960.

Mile 69.5 - This is a large group, all equipped with bicycles. Their SWAG wagon was parked on Canal Road. There were also a couple of Boy Scout troops at this campsite.

Mile 69 - Boy Scout Troop 922, from Havre de Grace, Maryland, takes a break to fish near Antietam Creek Aqueduct. Their bike trip from Cumberland to Georgetown was a "once-in-a-lifetime opportunity" for the boys, and for the adult Troop leaders alike.

BSA Pioneer Troop 1's 2000 High Adventure trip was a 184.5 mile bike ride down the historic Chesapeake and Ohio River Canal from its start in Cumberland, Maryland, to its endpoint in Washington, DC. Through scenic rural hills, past Civil War battlegrounds (below right), and into urban traffic.

Mile 69.4 - Antietam's Burnside Bridge

Mile 70-80   Antietam Creek to Taylor's Landing

This section is notable for its many river curves and beautiful scenic vistas. Miles 76-80 are reputed as "the best deepwater Bass fishing on the Potomac."

At mile 72.8, the towpath crosses under the Route 34 bridge to Shepherdstown, West Virginia. The charming Bavarian Inn sits on a cliff overlooking the river. In January 2000, Shepherdstown was in the international news when it hosted the Israeli-Syrian negotiations.

The Killiansburg Cave is located about mile 75.7. On September 16-18, 1862, hundreds of Sharpsburg citizens came here to seek refuge under these cliffs from the Battle of Antietam. The cave entrance is visible from the C&O Canal towpath.

Sharpsburg's Antietam National Battlefield is considered one of the finest examples of a Civil War battlefield and one of the best preserved battlefields in the nation. Antietam National Battlefield Visitor Center is one mile north of Sharpsburg on Rte. 65. The Visitor Center is open daily 8:30 a.m. to 6 p.m. from Memorial Day to Labor Day, and 8:30 a.m. to 5 p.m. the rest of the year. Special events are scheduled throughout the year at the battlefield. Especially popular are the 4th of July celebration with the Maryland Symphony Orchestra and fireworks on the Saturday closest to July 4th. The annual Sharpsburg Heritage Festival is held in mid September.

There are several hikes in campgrounds along the C&O canal near Sharpsburg. Three national parks and 2 state parks are within 12 miles of Sharpsburg.

Barron's C&O Canal Trail Store (mile 76) near Taylor's Landing is a popular resting point. C&O hikers, bikers, and Potomac boaters are encouraged to drop in for a refreshment, or to browse the literature, books, and assorted C&O Canal memorabilia.

Points of Interest

mile 70.8:   Miller's Sawmill (limited parking)
mile 72.8:   Lock 38, C&O Canal Park Headquarters
mile 72.8:   Shepherdstown, WV - food, shops, and motels
mile 75.3:   Killiansburg Cave campsite
mile 75.8:   Killiansburg Cave
mile 76.6:   Synder's Landing and boat ramp
mile 76.6:   Sharpsburg, MD
mile 76.6:   Jacob Rohrbach Inn B&B 877-839-4242 - 1 Mile
mile 76.7:   Barron's C&O Canal Museum and Country Store, located up the hill
mile 79.9:   Horseshoe Bend campsite
    The easiest way to reach the Sharpsburg area from Washington:
    Take I-270 North to Frederick
    At Frederick, follow I-70 West toward Hagerstown
    At Exit 29, take Route 65 South toward Sharpsburg
    Soon after passing the battlefield visitor center, make a right onto Rte 34

River Access / Boat Ramp:

mile 76.6:   Snyder's Landing

Mile 72.8 - Lockhouse 38 near Shepherdstown.

Mile 75.61 - Not too far past the Killiansburg Cave camp site is a series of caves.

On September 16-18, 1862, hundreds of Sharpsburg citizens came to the Killiansburg Caves to seek refuge under these cliffs from the Battle of Antietam. The cave entrance is visible from the C&O Canal towpath. Many of the caves are on private property and should not be accessed.

Mile 75.2 - Killiansburg Campground.

Mile 76.65 - Snyder's Landing and Boat Ramp

Mile 76 - Ice cream cones 75 cents? That's what the sign at Snyder's landing says and the arrow is pointing this way, to Barron's C&O Canal Hiker Biker Store. This is a must-visit. Besides having lots of cool liquid refreshments, there's a C&O Canal museum with many historic pictures of sights along the canal. The canal headquarters are still at the foot of the James Rumsey bridge. Open year round.

Two caves are found around milepost 75.5 near Snyder's Landing. Snyder's Landing Cave #1 is about 120 feet long. Snyder's #2 has three entrances which connect with great difficulty. The cave is mostly narrow crawlways. A large flowstone mass (right) can be found immediately inside the largest entrance.

Mile 79.41 - Lock 40 Flume. Like lock 39, there's no lockhouse or gate. It's a deep lock with well preserved stonework. Another feature of each lock is the wall which separates the two water levels. Although it is somewhat overgrown, you can see the wall is right where the gate closes. Because this lock and lock 39 are both so close to feeder dam 4, they both have sturdy bypass flumes.

Mile 80-105   Taylor's Landing to Jordan Junction

This section of the Canal and Potomac River is one of the more scenic, beautiful stretches because of the region's ruggedness. Hiking can be difficult and biking impossible in places, but you can reach wildlife and smallmouth bass fishing areas that are worth it.

Mile 84 through 88 is an impassable section of the C&O. There is a bicycle detour between Dam #4 and McMahon's Mill. There are several caves near Dam #4, and five cave openings known as Howell Cave are found in the limestone cliffs near McMahon's Mill.

Big Slackwater is between miles 85.5 and 88.1. The area is a widening and flattening of the Potomac River caused by Dam #4. This "slackwater" was used by C&O Canal barge boats with the river bank as the towpath, therefore there is no canal here. At mile 85.7 you will find a parking area, picnic tables, grills, chemical toilets, and a Boat Ramp.

Williamsport, Maryland highlights this section of the towpath. The town's Cushwa Basin at the C&O Canal was a major inland port during the late 1800's. Stores and restaurants are nearby. Just north of Cushwa Basin lies the Conococheague Aqueduct.

The main access for Williamsport is at Cushwa Basin. This is an extension of the canal that allowed boats access to the Cushwa Coal and other warehouses at Williamsport. The Cushwa Warehouse is now the C&O Canal Visitor Center. The oldest portion of this building is believed to have been constructed between 1790 and 1810, and may have replaced an earlier warehouse. The Basin and the warehouse building was named Cushwa around 1880 when it was owned by Victor Cushwa.

Points of Interest

mile 81.0:	Taylor's Landing boat ramp
mile 82.5:	Big Woods campsite
mile 84-88:	Towpath detour
mile 84.4:	Dam #4. Picnic area; several caves nearby
mile 85.7:	Big Slackwater
mile 86.7:	Detour from towpath
mile 88:	Howell Cave
mile 88.1:	McMahon's Mill; end bike detour
mile 88.1:	Detour from towpath
mile 88:	Big Slackwater
mile 90.9:	Opequon Junction campsite
mile 94.4:	Falling Waters
mile 95.2:	Cumberland Valley campsite
mile 99.3:	Williamsport, Cushwa Basin
mile 100:	Conocochengue Creek Aqueduct
mile 105:	Jordan Junction campsite

River Access / Boat Ramp

mile 81:	Taylor's Landing
mile 85.7:	Big Slackwater
mile 99.3:	Cushwa Basin, Williamsport

Mile 81 - At this point the canal opens up from the cliffs and steep Potomac river bank to an almost level passage through Mercersville. This is a picture of Taylor's landing which is your standard issue boat ramp. Take a close look at the red stripe down the middle of the ramp. It's an indicator of water levels on the Potomac.

Mile 82.46 - Big Woods campground. This campsite is more private than many of the others along the canal so. It's not visible from the canal but there's a little path (clearly marked with an NPS sign) that leads to this camping area.

Mile 84.4 - Although the gate is now missing, this winch house at Dam 4 was used to raise and lower a gate for protection against floods. The gate fit across the canal directly beneath the winch house.

Howell Caves
at mile 88

Mile 85.4 - The Potomac near Dam 4.

Mile 85.8 - Past the Big Slackwater parking lot and boat launch is the guard lock for Dam 4. Here boats would leave the canal and be pulled along the river using the riverbank as the towpath. The canal stops here and doesn't reappear until lock 41 at mile 88.9. It was the dam itself that caused the slack water.

Mile 86.7 - The cliffs start here and it is time to either head back or prepare for a tough hike. There is the remains of a towpath here but at certain parts you're really walking along the river bank. What's left of the towpath is badly overgrown with nettles and weeds.

Towpath Detour - Due to damage caused by repeated flooding, the towpath between the Dam #4 inlet lock and McMahon's Mill is closed until further notice. The detour is a distance of approximately 5 miles and is over narrow paved roads with no shoulders and limited sight distances. Those using the detour should do so with extreme caution. The map shows the route of the detour.

Dam #4 cave (also called Bear Cave) is an impressive-looking cave with a large, obvious, "Hollywood" entrance (below). In wet weather a stream emerges from the cave. The total

Mile 88.1 - This very picturesque mill at McMahon's Mill was operated by a paddle wheel. The brook still

Mile 88.9 - Lock 41 at Dam 4.

Big Slackwater

Mile 88.5 - Towpath along Big Slackwater area.
The C&O Canal has not yet resumed.

Feeder Dam No. 4 lies at Mile 84.4 on
the canal. This dam is in good condition, and fishermen frequent the rocks
in the river just below the dam. The
dam impounds the river so that the
next few miles upriver make a long
lake, called "Big Slackwater." This is
also the point at which a detour from
the towpath begins. Over the next few
miles there is no separate canal, as
"Big Slackwater" was found sufficient
for navigation. The towpath through
this stretch of river is the riverbank itself, which for part of the distance lies
at the foot of cliffs. In any sort of high
water, some of this section of towpath
will be under water.

FALLING WATERS

RETREATING AFTER GETTYSBURG, THE
CONFEDERATE ARMY WAS TRAPPED FOR
SEVEN DAYS BY THE SWOLLEN POTOMAC
RIVER. JULY 13TH–14TH GEN. LEE WITH
LONGSTREET'S AND HILL'S CORPS CROSSED
HERE ON A PONTOON BRIDGE. EWELL'S
CORPS FORDED THE POTOMAC ABOVE
WILLIAMSPORT.

MARYLAND CIVIL WAR CENTENNIAL COMMISSION

Mile 94.44 - There are two large
stone foundations on either side
of the towpath.

Where there is water, there should
be turtles. The Canal around Lock
44 has lots of them. These three
(and four more nearby) were
large - about one foot long. They
were so moss-covered one could
barely identify them.

Mile 99.3 - A local artist sketches Lockhouse 44 at Williamsport in pastels.

Mile 99.3 - Lock 44 at Williamsport. This lock has recently been completely restored. The green fire retardant on the lock gates is a new NPS addition. That's not usual for 19th century construction. This lock house is a big one. The lockhouse was built several years after the C&O Canal was completed, and is different from almost all other lockhouses along the Canal. This section of the Canal is rewatered for approximately eight miles.

Mile 99.72 - Cushwa's Coal and Brick is now a C&O Visitor's Center. The basin is in the foreground. This is the main access at Williamsport, on Rte 11. Parking and the Conococheague Aqueduct are on the left (north). Supply boats could pull right up to the warehouses at the basin to load and unload their cargo. August annual Canal Days at Williamsport Cushwa Basin is an event for the entire family.

Mile: 99.8 - Conococheague Aqueduct (No. 5). The right side of the aqueduct was destroyed in 1920, when it was hit by a canal boat. A wooden wall was constructed in its place, which was used until the canal closed in 1924.

Mile 100 - 106 - There's a long stretch with no significant landmarks, just miles and miles and more miles.

Mile 105-115   Jordan Junction to Licking Creek

This section can be quite difficult to ride. The towpath is a coarse gravel base, unlike the smooth clay/gravel mixture found previously. The towpath follows along Interstate 70, with expected levels of interstate highway noise. The parallel Western Maryland Rail Trail (WMRT) has just been completed between mile 112 and 124, which may provide a pleasant and quieter alternative to the C&O Canal. The 12-mile trail runs parallel to the C&O Canal Towpath between Big Pool and Hancock. It is owned by Department of Natural Resources (DNR) and run by the staff at Fort Frederick State Park.

Several small caves and solution holes are developed in the bluffs along the C & O Canal, south of Two Locks. The northernmost cave is a 4-foot square opening in the cliff face, 20 feet above the river. It consists of a single room 10 feet in diameter and 5 feet high. The entrance to the largest cave is 150 feet to the south, 30 feet above the river. Four Locks marks one of the few spots were the canal strays from the Potomac River Basin. This is also the location of a Park Ranger Station. Fort Frederick State Park, located nearby, was used for various purposes between the French and Indian and the Civil Wars. There are exhibits, and an orientation film. A few hundred feet East on the South side of Rte. 56 is a dirt road that leads to an abandoned quarry with fossils. South on McCoy's Ferry Road leads to a campground and park.

Fort Frederick State Park has recreation facilities including boat rentals and a launch. Just west of Fort Frederick is the Big Pool area. Big Pool Lake was constructed as an alternative to digging the canal basin. The Big Pool area is a popular destination for hiking, camping, fishing, boating, and for its beautifully scenic walks. Big Pool, Fort Frederick State Park, and the WMRT are easily accessed from Maryland, Virginia, the District, and southwestern Pennsylvania.

Maryland DNR Fisheries Restoration and Enhancement Programs stocked 4,250 rainbow trout in Big Pool in the spring of 2002.

Rewatered Section of the C&O Canal

Big Pool at mile 112 is completely rewatered, and offers opportunities for boating, fishing, and watching or photographing aquatic wildlife.

Points of Interest

mile 106.8:   Charles Mill
mile 106.5:   Feeder Dam # 5
mile 107.2:   Two Locks; several small caves
mile 108.6:   Four Locks Ranger Station and Recreation Area; picnic area
mile 109.6:   North Mountain campsite; water
mile 110.4:   McCoy's Ferry Recreation Area; RV Parking available
mile 112.4:   Fort Frederick State Park; camping
mile 112.5:   Begin Western Maryland Rail Trail (WMRT) to Hancock, 12 miles; this can be a pleasant alternative to the towpath
mile 112.5:   Big Pool Junction

River Access / Boat Ramp

Four Locks Ranger Station, m. 108.6, McCoy's Ferry Recreational Area, m. 110.4; Fort Frederick State Park, m. 112.4

Mile 106.8 - At Feeder Dam #5 there's a plaque that reads:
Floods occur at regular intervals in the Potomac Valley. Between 1829 and 1998, there have been 144 recorded floods or high water occurrences. Repairing flood damage was a continuing battle for the C & O Canal Company and is still a problem for the National Park Service. During periods of low water, the remains of the original crib and rubble dam, destroyed by floods, can be seen downstream from the present dam built in 1857.

In 1998, the guard lock and flume were filled with soil to halt the collapse of the stone walls. A section of towpath that was collapsing was replaced with "Roller Compacted Concrete (RCC)" which is a concrete mix with a small amount of cement and a high amount of gravel. The stone for the aggregate was acquired locally to the match the stone already used here. The RCC is spread and compacted by a roller and does not require formwork like conventional concrete. By filling the lock and bypass flume, and reconstructing the towpath and guard dike, the National Park Service is trying to protect the historical structures here from future flood damage. (A daunting task, at best.)

Mile 106.8 - Dam No. 5. The towpath rests on a concrete platform. This is what the plaque referred to as the "towpath and guard dike." If you stop by the Williamsport Visitor Center, you can see a photo of the stone wall it replaced.

This is the inlet lock that was filled in. Canal traffic from here to Lock 45 was routed to slackwater along the Potomac River via this lock. Since the Canal was closed and barge traffic halted in 1924, there was no need to "maintain" Canal facilities, even though many of the lockhouses have been maintained. When preservation of the C&O Locks became a concern in the 1960's, and especially with the takeover by the National Park Service in 1972, most of the C&O Canal locks and aqueducts have benefited from maintenance and preservation programs. In many sections, however, restoration of serious storm damage to facilities has not been performed.

Mile 107 - You can see why this section of the canal is missing, the cliffs come so close to the edge of the water, there was no place to build it. This section of the towpath is made of Roller Compacted Cement.

Mile 107.27 - Lock 45 marks the return of the canal and the towpath crosses over to the other side of the Canal. This is an inlet lock, providing access to the river, near Feeder Dam #5.

Mile 107.42 - This lock and lock 45 make up "Two Locks" and the lockhouse you see here served both. The stone structure to the right of the lockhouse was the foundation of a crossover bridge that took the towpath to the other side in preparation of entering the Potomac at Lock 45.

Mile 108.8 - Four Locks. The canal takes a shortcut here across Prather's Neck and leaves the side of the Potomac for an overland route. Consequently, four locks are required to handle the sudden change in elevation. This is a view of lock 49 with lock 50 in the background.

Left: Mile 108.8 - This is a view of lock 50 with lock 49 in the background.
Right: Mile 108.13 - There's a plaque on the towpath that reads: The first evidence of a mill here was in 1790. The mill was typical of grist mills which sprang up in this area to serve farmers in the surrounding countryside. Grain and flour could be loaded onto canal boats right from the mill. This property had been in the Charles family since the mill was built. The mill closed after the 1924 flood which ended the commercial life of the canal.

Mile 110.29 - From Four Locks to this point and beyond, the canal has a stone wall. This structure leads to a long creek and then the river. It may have been used to control the water level.

Mile 108.8 - The Four Locks

McCoy's Ferry Fossils
off Rte 56 on McCoy's Ferry Road
(301) 739-4200

From Hancock take I-70 East and exit at Route 56, bear right. Continue past Ft. Frederick State Park to a right turn onto McCoy's Ferry Road. Proceed under railroad bridge and park. Fossils can be found in the road cut near the railroad bridge. A large fauna is dominated by the brachiopods, pelecypods and gastropods. Look for more fossils at the base of one of the bridge supports.

Mile 110.42 - This is a large picnic, camping and boating park at North

Mile 112.5 to Mile 113.94 - Big Pool is more of a small lake. It is stocked with Rainbow Trout and circled with fisherman trails. Just west of Fort Frederick State Park, Big Pool Lake was constructed to reduce the amount of digging required for the canal basin.

Mile 112.40 - Fort Frederick is a French and Indian War stone fort, one of the best preserved in the U.S. It is restored to its 1758 appearance. Built in 1756 to protect frontiersman during the French and Indian Wars, The fort was a refuge for settlers and a base for military operations.
The shape of the fort is designed for maximum defense. Each of the four corners jut out into an arrowhead to provide a platform for shooting anyone attempting to scale the walls.

Western Maryland Rail Trail (WMRT)

The Western Maryland Rail Trail protects cultural and natural resources by buffering the C&O Canal National Historic Park and the adjacent Potomac River. Rich in history, the Western Maryland Line provided an avenue for early commerce. The first trail marker is located at Big Pool Junction.

Beginning approximately one-half mile west of historic Fort Frederick State Park in Washington County, Maryland, the Western Maryland Rail Trail (WMRT) winds along the Potomac River through rolling farmland, woodlands, and rural towns to its terminus at Pennsylvania Avenue in downtown Hancock, Maryland.

The second part of a three-phase project, a 9.5 mile long, 10-foot wide paved trail was constructed with gravel shoulders along the old Western Maryland Railway right-of-way in the city of Hancock. The route connects with the first phase, a 10.5 –mile trail that begins at Fort Frederick. The final phase will add 2.5 miles to the trail and a 50-vehicle terminus parking lot to complete the Hiker-Biker Trail.

Common activities people enjoy on the trail include hiking, biking, jogging, and roller blading. The easy grade and paved surface make this path ideal for families, the elderly and persons with disabilities to enjoy a trek outside.

Big Pool Junction

The Big Pool Train Station was constructed in 1892 to make a connection with the B&O Railroad across the river at Cherry Run, West Virginia. The Western Maryland Railroad was in a boom stage of growth with the 18 miles of rail between Hagerstown and Big Pool being the busiest section on the railway. In the spring of 1904 the building of the Cumberland Extension began at Big Pool. The Western Maryland reached Hancock by December of that year and Cumberland by March two years later.

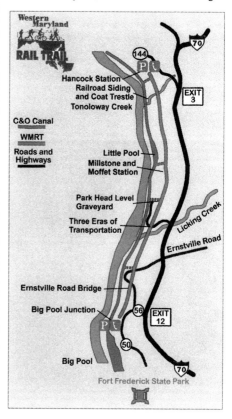

Ernstville Road Bridge

The Ernstville Road Bridge was constructed in 1930 to carry motor vehicles on Ernstville Road safely over the Western Maryland Railway. The present concrete culvert overpass was constructed in 1997 as part of the development of the Western Maryland Rail Trail. *2.1 miles to Licking Creek Bridge.*

Three Eras of Transportation

Facing west, Licking Creek Aqueduct is visible to the left. Constructed between 1836 and 1838, this is a single-arch aqueduct built of limestone. This 90-foot span is the longest of the C&O Canal's six single-arch aqueducts. The coming of the railroad industry put an end to the usefulness of canals. To the right is the Interstate 70 bridge over Licking Creek. *Only 0.3 miles to the next stop.*

Park Head Level Graveyard

Near this site is located a graveyard that dates to the early 1800's. There are numerous marked and unmarked graves. Plain field stones serve as common markers.

Millstone and Moffet Station

A small community originally called Millstone Point, but later simplified to just Millstone, grew up along the Chesapeake and Ohio Canal in this area. During the Civil War several companies of the first Regiment Maryland Infantry were stationed at Millstone Point to protect the C&O Canal from Confederates. The Moffet Station was constructed nearby when the Cumberland Extension of the Western Maryland Railway came through this location. *A mile to scenic Little Pool.*

Little Pool

Little Pool, a pretty body of water, nearly one mile long, was part of the Chesapeake and Ohio Canal. The pool and adjacent wooded areas are excellent for birding. A wooden foot bridge near the eastern end of Little Pool connects the Western Maryland Rail Trail and the C&O Towpath. *3.8 miles to marker #7.*

Railroad Siding and Coal Trestle

A railroad siding was constructed near here to allow engineers to unload their cargo at the coal trestle, simplifying the handling of this valuable resource. *0.2 miles of trail left.*

Hancock Station

The Hancock Station was a combination passenger and freight station that was constructed from 1904-1905. Passenger service was disconnected in the early 1950's. To reach the eastern end of the Western Maryland Rail Trail, take exit 12, MD 56, from I-70. Turn east and go to Big Pool. The trail parking lot is across the street from the Post Office.

To reach the western end of the Western Maryland Rail Trail, take exit 3 from I-70 into Hancock. Travel west on MD 144 for 1.4 miles. Turn left into Rail Trail parking.

112.5 - Big Pool. Instead of constructing a canal at this point, the engineers created a lake using a natural ridge.
Below: The upper end of Big Pool (Mile 113.9). This is a popular boating and fishing area, and the scenic beauty is worth the visit.

Mile 115-130   Licking Creek to Leopard's Mill

Winding from Little Pool to Hancock, the river moves out of the more mountainous areas of the Ridge and Valley Province and into the Great Valley, sometimes considered a separate province. Here the river meanders through the valley, embraced on its sides by both the railroad and the canal. A wonderful river stretch for casual canoeing, the area also offers good fishing, especially Yellow and White Perch and Crappie.

Little Pool at mile 120 is completely rewatered and offers a boat ramp, camping and fishing. Nearly a mile long, Little Pool and the adjacent wooded areas are excellent for birding. A wooden foot bridge near the eastern end of Little Pool connects the 12 mile paved Western Maryland Rail Trail beginning near Fort Frederick State Park, and the C&O towpath. The Hiker-Biker campsite at Little Pool does not have vehicle access. Located Near I-70, the campsite may be subject to noise.

The town of Hancock, Maryland highlights this section of the canal. In the mid 1800's, Hancock was a major inland port because of the C&O Canal. At mile 124, Hancock makes a great overnight stop when hiking or biking the entire canal. Restaurants, stores, and lodging are within a mile of the Canal. A nearby abandoned limestone quarry boasts numerous fossils with its rock and rubble.

The Tuscarora Trail terminates in Hancock after originating at the Appalachian Trail near Duncannon, Pennsylvania. Here the Tuscarora connects to the Big Blue Trail system, a 142.3 mile trail that runs from Hancock to the Appalachian Trail in Shenandoah National Park, Virginia. This is an "easy ride" trail. While riding or hiking the trail overnight, you are required to stay at designated campsites.

Other points of interest in this section include the single arch Licking Creek Aqueduct, said to have the largest stone arch in the U.S., and the Tonoloway Creek Aqueduct ruins. The Round Top Cement ruins are a few brick walls, the smokestack and the main chambers of eight cement kilns. The Round Top Cement ruins hide numerous abandoned limestone mines and several small caves along the railroad cuts and the C&O Canal.

Maryland DNR Fisheries Restoration and Enhance Programs stocked 2,500 rainbow trout in Licking Creek and 500 rainbow trout in Little Tonoloway Creek in the spring of 2001, and again in 2002.

Points of Interest

mile 116.4:   Licking Creek Aqueduct; camping; water
mile 121.0:   Little Pool; camping; water
mile 122.9:   Tonoloway Creek Aqueduct
mile 124.0:   End Western Maryland Rail Trail (WMRT)
mile 124.1:   Hancock, MD - Stores, restaurants, motels, museums
mile 124.1:   Tuscarora Trail
mile 126.5:   White Rock campsite; water
mile 127.4:   Round Top Cement Mill; food; several caves

River Access / Boat Ramp:

mile 120:   Little Pool
mile 124.0:   Hancock

Mile 116.04 - A single arch aqueduct is at Licking Creek. The wall on the upstream side has fallen away. Although the canal goes through some remote areas, from Big Pool to Hancock it runs along side Interstate 70 and the traffic noise is comparable to the sections close to Washington, DC.

Mile 119 - Little Pool. A culvert takes the overflow under the canal and out to the Potomac.

Little Pool

Mile 122.59 - Lock 51. The towpath from Roundtop to Tonoloway Ridge is severely damaged for substantial stretches (miles 127-133). The damage is sporadic enough that you can walk your bike over the worst spots.

Mile 122.59 - Lock 51 near Tonoloway Creek.

Mile 122.96 - This is a single arch aqueduct. The side on the left rests on rocks and is much higher than the right side which goes all the way to the bank of the Tonoloway. Since both sides of the aqueduct are gone, a bridge with handrails has been built.

Mile 124.1 - C&O Canal and trail in Hancock. The canal contributes to flooding in Hancock. The aqueducts plug with debris causing flooding.

Western MD Outdoor Festival & Bike Festival

June 14-15, 2003. Great food, entertainment, activities. Contact the cochairmen of the event for additional details: Lou Close (301-678-5389) or John Norris (301-678-6705).

Annual Hancock Days Festival

Hancock sponsors the Annual Hancock Days Festival at the beginning of August. The shops and stores of Hancock were decked out with special displays, exhibits and attractions.

Canal Apple Days

The 26th annual Canal-Apple Days in Widmeyer Park on Main Street. Activities begin on Saturday, September 14, 2002 with the Grand Parade through Hancock at 11 am. There's arts & crafts, food vendors for all tastes, a baby contest, antique/classic car displays, and more.

The Tonoloway lodge, Needmore, PA., an absolutely beautiful place to stay. Convenient to DC and Baltimore. (410) 636-2366 e-mail: barb@mountainlodge.com.

Hancock Winter Festival

The Arts Council of Hancock builds a small mountain of snow in Widmeyer Memorial Park, whether is snows or not! Exact dates and times will be posted on the Events Calendar.

e-mail: info@HancockMD.com

The Tuscarora Trail

The Rag-Tag Rangers photographed this view of the Potomac at Hancock from the Tuscarora Trail. They are a loosely organized outdoor group that likes to hike and backpack in the Mid-Atlantic states. They have been doing it since 1995. All are welcome to their treks.

Mile 127.4 - The cement kilns at Roundtop, near Hancock. Portland Cement, invented in 1824, was made by burning finely ground chalk with finely divided clay in a lime kiln until carbon dioxide was driven off. The sintered product was then ground to a powder. In 1845, the material that emerged from the cement kiln after high-temperature burning, called clinkers, was in the form of dark porous nodules. Theses were ground with a small amount of gypsum to produce cement.

Mile 130-150   Leopard's Mill to Stickpile Hill

This section is one of the most remote areas along the entire canal. The mountainous terrain provides wonderful scenic vistas, with very limited access. The only town in this section is Little Orleans, which is just four or five buildings. There are six Hiker/Biker campsites in this section, and the Little Orleans Campground and Park Area. The campground has a playfield, swimming pools, a game room, and a camp store. The RV site has electric, water and sewer hook ups.

Sideling Hill Creek is the border between Allegany and Washington counties. From its start on the mountain slopes of southwestern Pennsylvania, Sideling Hill Creek meanders southward through narrow farming valleys and below steep, wooded ridges before joining the Potomac River. Amid the peacefulness of this undisturbed land are habitats supporting species seldom found elsewhere, such as the rare Olympia Marble butterfly. Wild turkey, hawks, and bobcats share the rugged terrain. The creek is known to trout fishermen who enjoy catching rainbows stocked there by state hatchery crews.

The town of Little Orleans is famous for its General Store, and the campground located on the canal nearby. Little Orleans was once located on the main route from Fort Frederick to Cumberland, but is only accessible now by winding back roads.

Maryland DNR Fisheries Restoration and Enhancement Programs stocked 8,500 rainbow trout in Sideling Creek, and 8,500 rainbow trout in Fifteenmile Creek in the spring of 2001, and again in 2002.

Points of Interest

mile 129.9: Leopard's Mill; camping; water
mile 130.9: Irishman's Lock 53
mile 131.3: Roadbridge over Canal to Cohill Station and boatramp
mile 133.6: Cacapon Junction campsite; water
mile 134.2: Polly Pond
mile 134.2: Long Hollow at Polly Pond
mile 134.2: Dam No. 6
mile 136.6: Sideling Hill Creek Aqueduct
mile 139.2: Indigo Neck campsite; water
mile 140.8: Little Orleans - General Store; water
mile 140.8: Fifteenmile Creek Recreation Area (drive-in campground)
mile 140.9: Fifteenmile Creek Aqueduct; food
mile 144.5: Devil's Alley and campsite; water
mile 149.4: Stickpile Hill and campsite; water

River Access / Boat Ramp

mile 131.3: Cohill Station
mile 140.8: Little Orleans/Fifteen Mile Creek, about a 1-¾ hour drive from the Washington Beltway. Take I-270 North to Frederick, MD. Take I-70 West to Hancock, MD.

Mile 129.96 - Lock 53, Irishman's Lock

Mile 130.8 - Leopard's Mill was a cement mill that operated before Roundtop. These mills sprang up where there were sufficient limestone deposits. It's not clear what this structure is but it's across the canal in a nearby stream that was possibly used to power the mill.

Cacapon

Long Hollow at Polly Pond is a really beautiful place. Only about two miles from the Sideling Creek area and major highways, this is a quiet, little-known hideaway that is well worth the visit.

Mile 136.56 - From above the Sideling Hill Creek Aqueduct, atop the railroad bridge, you can see the missing upstream wall, a rather common site for an aqueduct. It is a single arch. Sideling Hill Creek Aqueduct (No. 8), completed in 1848; a single span of 110 feet. This creek marks the border between Washington County and Allegany County.

Mile 140.8 - This is a rather significant spot as it's almost the last spot accessible by major roads until Cumberland. Bill's bar has become a landmark but in 2000 it burned down. The soda machines still work. Just down the road there are campsites for both group and individual camping, a boat launch and parking.

Mile 140.9 - Fifteenmile Creek Aqueduct. Very similar to nearby Sideling Creek Aqueduct, it's a single arch with the upstream wall missing.

Mile 143.96 - Lock 58. There are no stones; the lock is covered with concrete. This is the first of thirteen locks so constructed. The walls of the canal were originally covered with lumber because of the shortage of finishing stones in the area.

An 1841 map listed a site near Devil's Alley as the "Carroll's Steam Saw Mill." It was built in 1836, and financed from the estate of Charles Carroll of Carrollton, who was one of the signatories of the Declaration of Independence. Along with the saw mill, there was also a grist mill, a blacksmith shop, stables, and quarters for workmen. Logs were processed here and then sent 1.25 miles down Devil's Alley, where they were then transported by canal and railroad to Washington and Baltimore.

144.54 - Devil's Alley hiker-biker campsite.

Mile 150-170   Stickpile Hill to Pigman's Ferry

Just two miles south and east of Oldtown, the South Branch joins the North Branch and the Potomac completes its transformation from high mountain stream to a wider, slower-moving river. Further on, the river moves into a series of sharp turns referred to as the Paw Paw bends.

Here the C&O Canal Company built the Paw Paw Tunnel, the single most impressive engineering feature on the canal. Located between mile 155 and 156, the 3118-foot-long tunnel was finished in 1850 and was the final link from the Chesapeake Bay to Cumberland. Expected to be completed in about 18 months, it took 14 years to complete. At 24 feet high, it is the largest man-made structure on the C&O Canal. The tunnel is lined with more than 6 million bricks.

The Paw Paw Tunnel is very long and very dark; flashlights are more than suggested. There is a sturdy walkway and railing that overlooks steep rockface drops, and at the same time is dwarfed by the towering rock walls. After leaving the south tunnel portal, the towpath passes the Paw Paw camping area, and goes under Route 51. The town of Paw Paw, West Virginia is a mile down Route 51, and has food, shops, and lodging. The Paw Paw Tunnel Trail, from mile post 155 to mile post 156, is a two-mile hiker-bike trail.

Other points of interest include the Town Creek Aqueduct (restored in 1977) and a fully restored section of the canal at the historic area called Oldtown. The Warrior's Path passed through this area, predating the history of the United States.

Maryland DNR Fisheries Restoration and Enhancement Programs stocked 4,000 rainbow trout in Battie Mixon's Fishing Pond, and 4,000 in Flintstone Creek in the spring of 2001. In the spring of 2002, 3,500 rainbow trout were stocked in Battie Mixon's Fishing Pond, 3,500 rainbow trout in Flintstone Creek, and 8,000 rainbow trout in Rocky Gap Lake.

Rewatered Section of the C&O Canal
Miles 162 through 167 around Town Creek are completely rewatered, and offer opportunities for boating, fishing, and watching or photographing aquatic wildlife.

Points of Interest
mile 150:	Green Ridge State Forest
mile 152:	Rocky Gap State Park
mile 154.1:	Sorel Ridge and campground
mile 155.2:	Paw Paw Tunnel and campground
mile 156.2:	Paw Paw, WV
mile 157.4:	Purslane Run
mile 162.3:	Town Creek
mile 162.4:	Battie Mixon's Fishing Spot
mile 164.8:	Potomac Forks
mile 166.4:	Twigg's Lock
mile 166.7:	Oldtown
mile 169.2:	Pigman's Ferry campsite; water

River Access / Boat Ramp
mile 152:	Bonds Landing at Green Ridge State Park

Green Ridge State Forest
28700 Headquarters Drive, NE, Flintstone, Maryland 21530
(301) 478-3124

The Green Ridge State Forest, the second largest of Maryland's state forests, stretches across several mountains of Western Maryland, including Town Hill, Polish Mountain, and Green Ridge Mountain. The forest facilities include campsites, boat launching areas, picnic facilities, and riding trails. There is a small craft launching area at Bond's Landing. A permit, available for a small service charge, is required for camping in the forest. The forest has a handicap-accessible hunting program and a shooting range.

The forest is known for its population of white-tailed deer, wild turkey, and squirrel, along with ruffled grouse, cottontail rabbit, quail, and fox. Fishing is on the Potomac and Fifteenmile Creek, Town Creek, Sideling Hill Creek, Orchard Pond, and White Sulphur Pond. These creeks and ponds are stocked with trout each spring. Parts of these streams and ponds are designated trout streams and are subject to "put and take" regulations by the Maryland Department of Natural Resources.

Vacationers can access numerous biking, hiking, snowmobiling, and ORV trails. There are approximately 100 primitive campsites throughout the forest, and fishing in the Potomac, hunting in the fall, and shooting ranges for clay for the skeet outdoor sportsman. There are over 27 miles of hiking trails that trace narrow ridges and stream valleys in the forest. The trail connects with the C&O Canal towpath, providing a 46-mile circuit hike. Green Ridge State Forest offers canoeing in the eastern part of Allegany County. A boat ramp here provides easy access to the Potomac River, a waterway rich in the history of colonial and 19th century Maryland. The Green Ridge State Forest headquarters are open 8 a.m. to 4 p.m., 7-days a week in spring, summer, and fall.

Nature Tourism - Guided Adventures
The Nature Tourism staff works with Maryland's outdoor guides and outfitters to introduce more people to Nature Tourism experiences, including: canoeing, kayaking, bicycling, hunting, rock climbing, historical tours, rappelling, watchable wildlife, fishing, guided ORV tours, rafting and backpacking. The State Forest and Park Service is improving trail and camping access, information guides, maps and brochures to enable visitors to better enjoy outdoor adventures. To schedule a Nature Tourism adventure while visiting Green Ridge State Forest, call 301-784-8403.

The Trail Stewardship Program
You can help support trails at your favorite forest or park by purchasing a Trail Stewardship Sticker at the Green Ridge Visitor Center. Your donation supports resources to maintain and construct trails in the forest or park of your choice.

Green Ridge Mountain Bike Trails
There are over 20 miles of trail and probably 100 more of forest roads in undulating terrain that mixes single and doubletrack. The Maryland State Mountain Bike Championships have been held here.

Green Ridge State Forest Fall Color Driving Tour

This self-guided tour can be enjoyed not only in the fall, but year-round, and the tour route is approximately 30-miles long. The tour takes about three hours to complete. The Green Ridge State Forest office is located 8 miles east of Flintstone, MD at Exit 64 (M.V. Smith Road) off I-68. For additional information and for a map call the state forest office at 301-478-3124. Depending on the time of year, the roads could be dusty, muddy, full of ruts and strewn with rocks.

Mile 0

Begin your tour at Green Ridge State Forest headquarters. As you exit the headquarters, return to I-68 and proceed west to Exit 62. At the end of this exit, turn left. You are now heading south on 15 Mile Creek Road. Shale soils and exposed rock on the hillsides adjacent to the road on the right have a "ripple" appearance. These rocks were created when the surface was exposed to the ocean floor millions of years ago. Over the next few miles you will see trees such as the white pine, white oak, and red maple. Ahead you will cross over White Sulphur Run, a tributary of 15 Mile Creek. From that point you will begin to experience the steep ascents and descents that are typical of the Ridge and Valley Province.

Mile 2.1

Turn left and continue along 15 Mile Creek Road. You will soon be crossing another tributary of 15 Mile Creek, which is known as Deep Run. Ahead there are numerous sharp bends.

Mile 3.4

Turn right into Stafford Road. This road is rough, so drive slowly. You are ascending the west side of Town Hill. As you climb this ridge, note that the red oak increases dramatically. In the lower elevations in moist sites, you will see white oak.

Mile 4.5

You are now 1,570 feet above sea level. From this vista, you have a splendid view of the surrounding landscape. To your right, you can see the Potomac River as it snakes lazily in the distance. The large ridge in the distance is Sideling Hill. The road will be one of the most difficult roads on your tour. Turn left onto Stafford Trail. Ahead, you will encounter an example of this region's sandstone cliff formations. From here, you will be descending down the east side of Town Hill.

Mile 5.7

Turn right onto Dug Hill Road. Just ahead (0.2 miles) you will make a left turn onto historic Oldtown Road. As a part of history, this road is considered to be one of the oldest roads in Allegany County, it was built in 1755 during the French and Indian War and connected Fort Frederick to Fort Cumberland. This also is the same road that connects Little Orleans with Oldtown.

Mile 6.8

Turn right onto Carroll Road. Approximately one quarter mile down and to your left, you can enjoy the view from "Point Lookout."

Mile 7.9

The sugar maple is a dominant tree in this area. Sugar maples thrive in areas of moisture and shade. As you bear right at the next form, you pass such features as Roby Run and Pignut Ridge. Off to the left you will see Roby Cemetery. Many of the old headstones in this clearing serve as monuments to some of this area's early settlers and their descendents. At mile 9.8 take a sharp turn left onto Kasecamp Road. Approximately a half mile ahead on the right you will see the Stickpile Tunnel.

Mile 13.7

Turn left at the entrance to Bond's Landing. Here you will cross a section of the C&O Canal. A parking lot and day use area have been provided. The road to your left leads to the camping area. Proceed back to the entrance and turn left onto Kasecamp Road.

Mile 14.2

This was the site of the Old Green Ridge Station of the Western Maryland Railroad. At the next intersection, turn left onto Mertens Avenue. Whitetail deer can often be spotted throughout this area. At mile 16.8, you start to climb Town Hill Mountain.

Mile 18

"Banner's" Overlook on top of Town Hill, which is 1,650 feet above sea level. Proceed along Mertens Avenue. From here, you will be descending Town Hill. At the power line crossing (mile 20), you are at the top of Green Ridge Mountain. Turn left onto Green Ridge Road, and proceed 2.2 miles to the "Log Roll" Overlook.

Mile 22.2

This scenic area is known as the "Log Roll." During the timbering era of the 1880's and 1890's, logs were dragged from the nearby hills to be rolled down these slopes into Town Creek below. The logs were then floated several miles to the sawmill. Three states can be seen from what many people feel is one of the most beautiful areas in Maryland. The mountains to your left are in West Virginia, the middle area is Maryland, and Pennsylvania is to your extreme right. You will now need to backtrack on Green Ridge Road, and proceed three miles past the power line crossing to the "Warrior Mountain" overlook.

Mile 27.7

Turn left onto Wallizer Road. One mile ahead on your right, you will see White Sulphur Pond. Once known as Finksburg (Mertensville), a large sawmill operation was located here during the 1880's. A large portion of the forest timber harvested during the later 19th century was cut at this mill. The Green Ridge logging railroad extended to this site.

Mile 30.2

Turn right onto Black Sulphur Road. One mile ahead you will make a right turn onto Williams Road. When you reach State Highway Route 144, turn right. After approximately one mile, you will be at the same exit where you began your tour.

The Green Ridge State Forest office is located 8 miles east of Flintstone, Maryland at Exit 64 (M.V. Smith Road) off I-68. For additional information call 301-478-3124.

Rocky Gap State Park
12500 Pleasant Valley Road NE
Flintstone, MD 21530
Oct-Apr: 8 am-dusk 7 days a week; May-Sep: 6 am-dusk 7 days a week
301-777-2139   1-888-432-CAMP (2267) for reservations

Handicap restrooms are available at the visitor center only. Rocky Gap offers a mobility impaired fishing dock, amphitheater, picnic tables and camping. The park offers two all-terrain chairs that are available to guests without charge.

Nature Tourism staff at Rocky Gap work with Maryland's outdoor guides and outfitters services to introduce more people to nature tourism experiences, including a handicap-accessible fishing dock, canoeing, kayaking, bicycling, hunting, rock climbing, historical tours, rappelling, watchable wildlife, rafting, fishing, and backpacking. To schedule a Nature Tourism adventure while visiting Rocky Gap State Park, call 301-784-8403.

Nestled in a natural saddle created by Evitts Mountain and Martin Mountain, this park offers mountain scenery and interesting hiking trails. Rocky Gap State Park encompasses over 3,000 acres of public land for guests to enjoy with three beaches; picnicking; boat rentals; hiking; golf; 243-acre lake for fishing; 278 camp sites; furnished rental chalet sleeps eight; educational programs; lodge, conference center; and golf resort. Rugged mountains surround the park which features 243-acre Lake Habeeb.

The lake is fed by Rocky Gap Run which winds its way through a mile long gorge displaying sheer cliffs, overlooks and a hemlock forest dense with rhododendron. Overlooking the lake is Evitts Mountain. Pets are allowed. Non-gas powered watercraft are allowed. Pontoon tours, rental canoes, rowboats, and paddleboats available Memorial day to Labor Day.

Three swimming beaches and a modern bathhouse adjoin a 243-acre lake and a large campground. Adventure Sports in the process of building an underwater diving/snorkeling venue at Rocky Gap. It will be the first of it's kind ever attempted in freshwater.

Camping
Rocky Gap offers 278 individual campsites, including 30 equipped with electric hookups, bathhouses, three youth group camping areas, two pavilions, one boat ramp, nature center, and a camp store. Pets are allowed in two designated camp loops. Ten mini-cabins, each with electric, bunk bed and a double bed, are available for rent. Check out a map of the park.

Mile 155.2 - The Paw Paw Tunnel took over 12 years to complete, and caused the Canal to lose the race with the railroad.

The cliffs over the tunnel are wet and dripping with water, just like inside the tunnel. There are a few hidden puddles and drippy spots, especially on the east side of the tunnel. A flashlight is a good idea.

Mile 162.34 - Town Creek Aqueduct (No. 10). One 100-foot span.

Mile 162.4 - Battie Mixon's Fishing Spot. A low concrete dam in the canal forms a fishing pond, the first of several such pools from here to Lock 71. This bird house by the pool was erected by the National Park Service.

Mile 165 - BSA Scout Troop 967 of Havre de Grace, Maryland riding on a typical section of trail below Oldtown, on their June 2000 bicycle trip from Cumberland, Maryland to Washington, DC on the C&O Canal Historical Trail. Scouts who have completed the entire C&O Canal trail qualify for the patch shown above; the segments around the perimeter represent the five councils of the Boy Scouts of America through which the C&O Canal trail passes.

Mile 166.44 - Twigg's Lock, Lock 69.

Mile 166.7 - Oldtown, Lock 70

Mile 170-184   Pigman's Ferry to Cumberland

The home stretch into Cumberland is mostly uneventful, except for the poor condition of the towpath. The path is soft in several places, resulting in ruts and mud holes. There was one section where the towpath became a single track trail cutting through backyards. Bikers can enjoy peddling to the North Branch picnic area from Cumberland for a 9.5 mile half-day round trip bike ride, or to Evitts Creek for a 4 mile ride.

The towpath ends at the Western Maryland Scenic Railroad Station and Canal Place, located just north of the Interstate 68 bridge. The canal itself was filled in back in the 1950's for flood control, so the towpath is all that remains. An upcoming waterfront revitalization project is expected to restore the canal to its formal glory.

Originally, the canal was supposed to continue farther northwest to Pittsburgh, thus joining the Ohio River to the Chesapeake Bay. By 1850, however, the railroad had won the race to open up the west, so further canal construction plans were scraped. Work has now been completed to connect Cumberland to Pittsburgh via a series of Rail-to-Trail projects. This 394-mile long greenway, the Great Allegheny Passage, now connects Washington, DC to Pittsburgh via the C&O Canal. Designated a National Recreation Trail, the Great Allegheny Passage enables hikers, bicyclists, cross-country skiers and people with disabilities to discover the region's beautiful river gorges and mountain vistas on a continuous hiker-biker trail.

Maryland DNR Fisheries Restoration and Enhancement Programs stocked 10,500 in Evitt's Creek in the spring of 2001, and another 9,500 rainbow trout in the spring of 2002. Almost 430,000 rainbows were stocked in nearly 100 Maryland streams, ponds and lakes in the spring of 2002.

Points of Interest

mile 173.3:   Spring Gap Recreation Area
mile 175.4:   Irons Mountain Campsite; water
mile 175.7:   North Branch; picnic area
mile 180.0:   Evitt's Creek campground; water
mile 180.7:   Evitt's Creek Aqueduct
mile 184.5:   Western Maryland Scenic Railroad
mile 184.5:   Cumberland, MD - restaurants, stores, lodging, entertainment

River Access / Boat Ramp:

mile 184.4:   Cumberland

Directions to Cumberland's Canal Place

Cumberland is about a two hour drive from the Washington Beltway.
Take I-270 North to Frederick, Maryland. Take I-70 West to Hancock, Maryland. Take I-68 West to Cumberland, Maryland.
In Cumberland, take Exit 43-C. At the bottom of the ramp, make left onto Harrison Street (at stop sign). The parking lot of TCI Cable and the Western Maryland Station Center is located at the end of the street. The Canal towpath begins directly to the left of the station (almost under the I-68 bridge).

Spring Gap

Mile 174.44 - Lock 72, The Narrows. This lock was named for the tight place between the river and the ends of Nicholas Ridge and Irons Mountains. It was also known as "Ten Mile Lock" as it is 10 miles from Cumberland.

Rose mallow, an endangered plant species of the Upper Potomac Subregion.

The canal finally enters the Cumberland city limits at Mile 180.75, near the last of the 11 aqueducts, which carries the canal over Evitt's Creek. The canal reaches its end at Mile 184.5, with the guard locks at Will's Creek. Evitt's Creek Aqueduct (No. 11), the last and the smallest aqueduct, with a single 70-foot span. Completed around 1840, the aqueduct has been stabilized in 1979 and 1983.

Mile 175.6 - Lock 75, the last lock. This is part of the North Branch set of locks. This two-foot bridge combination is common, with the first one over the canal and the second over the bypass flume.

Mile 180.7 - Evitt's Creek is the smallest of all 11 aqueducts. On the upstream side, parts of the wall have collapsed and are repaired only with plywood planks. There are Monocacy-Aqueduct-styled metal supports wrapped around the sides and underneath. The quality of the stonework done by Italian Stonemasons is still evident today. More amazing is the fact that this canal was dug by hand through ridge after ridge of rock. Scotch and Irish immigrants performed this task.

Cumberland, Maryland

Western Maryland Scenic Railroad

The restored early 20th century train steams through the mountains of Western Maryland on a 32 mile round trip between Cumberland and Frostburg from May through December. The trip covers a 1,300-foot change in elevation. You'll see tunnels and bridges, and catch glimpses of mountaintop scenery, and experience the rich transportation history.

Fort Cumberland Walking Trail

This walking trail covers several city blocks around the site of Fort Cumberland. A few hours or a full day can be spent appreciating the history of the fort and its garrison, the development of Cumberland, and the city's role in the development of our nation. A map of the trail is available at the Visitor's Information Center in the Western Maryland Station Center. Complete the walking trail and earn a special embroidered patch.

Meadow Mountain Trail

From Cumberland take I-68 to Exit 14 and on Route 219, head to Thayerville. Before crossing a bridge, take a left on Rock Ledge Road. Find State Park Road about 2.5 miles down. Another 2.5 miles, turn right on Waterfront Road, next a quick right, and park at the far end.

The C&O Canal terminus—now just a wide, grassy area beside the tracks and beneath eight lanes of a towering Interstate 68 overpass. In 2005 it will be magically transformed into Canal Place, a 45-million-dollar scheme to rewater the canal and offer barge rides, restaurants, shops, festival grounds, a museum, and a boatyard. You can visit the antiques, craft, and gift shops, and small restaurants of the pedestrian Downtown Mall, or the restored Western Maryland Station Center, a 1913 brick Victorian masterpiece, the National Park Service's C&O Canal Visitor Center, the Allegany County Visitor Center, and a restaurant and the Western Maryland Scenic Railroad.

Canalfest - Mid May
at the Canal Place Heritage Area

Celebrate Cumberland's C&O Canal Heritage and rich transportation history at the Annual C&O Canalfest - Cumberland. Period artisans, living history programs, excellent live entertainment, children's activities, canal boat replica tours, and many more exciting activities create an unforgettable weekend.

Following the Trails North

The C&O Canal National Historical Park trail is one of hundreds of interconnecting hiking trails from Georgia to Maine. Many of the trails are converted railroad lines, commonly known as Rails-To-Trails. The centerpoint of all of these trails is the Appalacian Trail, spanning 12 states and over 2,100 miles of the Eastern United States. The two other main trails that connect to the C&O Canal are the Tuscarora Trail, connecting Harrisonburg, Pennsylvania to the C&O Canal at Hancock, Maryland, and the Allegheny Highlands Trail of Maryland (AHTM) that connects Pittsburgh, Pennsylvania to Cumberland, Maryland.

The Appalachian Trail

The Appalachian National Scenic Trail is a 2,167-mile (3,488 km) footpath along the ridge crests and across the major valleys of the Appalachian Mountains from Katahdin in Maine to Springer Mountain in north Georgia. The trail traverses Maine, New Hampshire, Vermont, Massachusetts, Connecticut, New York, New Jersey, Pennsylvania, Maryland, West Virginia, Virginia, Tennessee, North Carolina and Georgia.

The Trail through Maryland is gentle, and is probably the easiest to hike, with no climbs over a thousand feet. It is recommended for novice hikers. You are required to stay at designated shelters and campsites. Other activities are available along the Trail in 6 units of the National Park Service, 8 national forests, and 60 state parks and forests.

Tuscarora Trail

The 110-mile Tuscarora Trail is the longest blue blaze on the Appalachian Trail. The terrain is rough and rocky. The Big Blue Trail is now part of the Tuscarora Trail, and extends for another 144 miles from the C&O Canal in Hancock, Maryland to the Appalachian Trail in the Shenandoah National Park at Matthews Arm in Virginia. The trail is well-traveled and maintained due to the determination of dedicated volunteers.

Great Allegheny Passage

On August 27, 1997, a national group designated the Pittsburgh-to-DC Trail as one of the 10 "most endangered" rail trails. U.S. Rep. John Murtha renewed his support for the Enhancements Program that supports trail development as part of the reauthorization of the federal transportation program. The Great Allegheny Passage is an alliance of seven rail to trail conversions in Western Maryland and Southwestern Pennsylvania. Designated a National Recreation Trail, the "GAP" enables hikers, bicyclists, cross-country skiers and people with disabilities to discover our region's beauty in river gorges, mountain vistas and sweeping cityscapes.

The Great Allegheny Passage covers 204 miles, of which 125 miles are constructed and heavily used. The trail system goes through five counties in Pennsylvania and one in Maryland. In Pennsylvania the "GAP" is comprised of the Three Rivers Heritage Trail; Steel Valley Trail; Montour Trail; Youghiogheny River Trail, North; Youghiogheny River Trail, South; and Allegheny Highlands Trails. At Cumberland, MD the ATA system connects with the 184.5-mile C&O Canal Towpath for a trip to Washington, DC.

The status of the 394-mile Pittsburgh-to-DC Trail follows:
- C&O Canal Towpath, Cumberland, MD, to Washington, DC, 184 miles.
- Allegheny Highlands Trail in Md., Cumberland to PA Line, 21 miles, planned.
- Allegheny Highlands Trail in Pennsylvania, PA Line to Confluence, 46 miles, 21 miles completed, and 25 miles planned.
- Youghiogheny River Trail South (Ohiopyle State Park), 28 miles, 26 miles completed from Boston to Connellsville.
- Youghiogheny River Trail North, 43 miles, complete. Surface of trail is crushed limestone. Accessible to people of all ages and all physical abilities.
- Montour Trail, 47 miles, 30 miles completed, 17 miles planned. Surface of trail is crushed limestone. Includes cross-country skiing.

The Allegheny Highlands Trail of Maryland (AHTM)
The Allegheny Highlands Trail of Maryland (AHTM) follows the route of the historic Western Maryland Railroad for 22 miles from Cumberland to the Pennsylvania line. From Cumberland to Frostburg the trail will parallel the Western Maryland Scenic Railroad and its steam locomotive. AHTM also designates the citizens' group that has promoted the development of the Maryland portion of the trail.

The Youghiogheny River Trail

This limestone surfaced trail was built along the "railbanked" right-of-way of the Pittsburgh & Lake Erie Railroad between McKeesport and Connellsville. The north section of trail has been completed from just north of Boston down to Connellsville and is open and to the public.

The trail continues to Confluence, PA for 66 miles of one of the most beautiful trails in the country. The trail is designed as a non-motorized, shared-use, recreational trail for bicycling, walking, fishing and canoe access, hiking, nature study, historic appreciation, cross country skiing, picnicking, and horseback riding. The trail is handicap accessible.

Nature and Activities
of the
C&O Canal Region

Birding the C&O Canal

The Potomac is an important migratory flyway, and the old C&O Canal, with its locks and ponds provides inviting habitat for migrants as well as breeding birds and other wildlife. At the peak of migration you may find more than 20 species of warblers here, as well as shorebirds, bitterns, waterthrushes, and swamp sparrows.

Pennyfield Lock

Pennyfield Lock is one of the locations along the old C&O Canal that is famous in birding circles. It's a beautiful place to bird—a walk (the old towpath) between canal and river, with trees and birds along a continuous edge over water. It can be terrific in spring migration, and a pleasure any time you're looking for a walk in nature. (Just keep alert for the cyclists that zoom up and down the path.)

Great Falls Park

Birdlife here takes advantage of the various habitats provided along the Potomac: floodplain woodlands, bedrock terraces, swamps, open areas, and upland deciduous forests. Birds of prey are continually aloft, and the woodpeckers, nuthatches, and chickadees of winter provide other viewing opportunities. On the Maryland side, eagles nest by the river above the parking lot; black crowned night herons fish below the falls at dusk.

Sycamore Island/Lock 7

Kingfishers, herons, cormorants, wood duck and black ducks are abundant. Osprey, caspian tern, and double-breasted cormorant, mallards, and a variety of woodpeckers such as downy, hairy, pileated, redbellied, and northern flicker are residents, and black-throated blue warblers, black-throated green, chestnut-sided, and american redstart frequent the area.

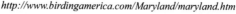

http://www.birdingamerica.com/Maryland/maryland.htm

Birdwatching at Pennyfield Lock

Belted Kingfisher

Baltimore Oriole

Prothonotary Warbler

Saw-Whet Owl

Wildlife of the Lower C&O Canal
and adjacent Potomac River

During the warm months, turtles bask on logs, dragonflies hunt insect prey. Out on the river, ducks and gulls feed, while great blue herons stalk the shallows. Many birds, such as warblers and osprey, migrate along the Potomac river valley. The big, showy pileated woodpecker is a year-round resident. At Great Falls, bald eagles are nesting again after an absence of 30 years from the upper Potomac. And almost anywhere on the 184-mile canal, you have a chance to see deer and beavers, swimming Turtles, Wood Ducks, Egrets, Belted Kingfishers, Osprey, and Great Blue Herons.

Red-eyed and White-eyed vireos, Great Crested Flycatcher, and warblers can be seen in the woods. Snowy and Great egrets, Great Blue Heron, Double Crested Cormorant, Fish Crow, Orange and Big bluets, and Blue Dashers can be seen near or on the river. Flowering plants attract Eastern Tiger Swallowtail, Silver-spotted Skipper, Red Admiral, and other butterflies.

Violette's Lock
Both Baltimore and Orchard Orioles—tropical migrants that are seen only in our region for three to four months per year, roughly May through August—nest in these trees. Most years a Red-shouldered Hawk pair nests somewhere nearby.

Seneca
You may find birds on the water—loons, grebes, cormorants, and an assortment of diving ducks. Frogs, water snakes, beavers, Green Herons and Osprey are found here. Years ago there were many standing dead trees in the water that were regularly visited by Prothonotary Warblers and Red-headed Woodpeckers, and are still occasionally seen.

Hughes Hollow
Red fox, gray fox, northern water snake, pickerel frog, spotted salamander, Northern Saw-whet Owl, Least Bittern, Willow Flycatcher, and the American Snout Butterfly just begin the long list of Hughes Hollow's wildlife.

Barred Owl

Sycamore Landing
Spring wildflowers are still plentiful and wildlife is common. Barred Owls inhabit the area and can frequently be seen.

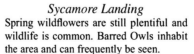

Wildlife of the Potomac Basin by Geologic Region

The Potomac River flows through ever-changing landscapes and sub-ecosystems, each with its own specific community of plants and animals. A trip along the river or the C&O Canal provides opportunity to see an abundance of birds, animals and butterflies. The river is categorized by three distinct geologic regions, each with its own types and varieties of plants and animals.

Flying Squirrel Dusky Salamander Rose-Breasted Grosbeak Harris' checkerspot *Allegheny Plateau*

Maryland Geologic Regions

Allegheny Plateau

Northern flying squirrels and black bears roam the hills and dusky salamanders may be found in niches and hollows on the cool, moist forest floor. Birds frequenting the area include the blackburnian warbler, rose-breasted grosbeak, and northern goshawk. Butterflies such as harris' checkerspot and the pink-edged sulphur may be found here.

Striped Skunk Long-Tailed Salamander Red-Tailed Hawk Northern Metalmark Smallmouth Bass

Ridge and Valley

Ridge and Valley

Animals found in these hills and valleys include bobcats, striped skunks and timber rattlesnakes. Long-tailed salamanders are found beneath rocks, decaying logs and in most areas beside mountain streams. Birders may see the chestnut-sided warbler, worm-eating warbler and red-tailed hawk. Butterflies include the aphrodite fritillary and northern metalmark. As the river drops from the heights of the Allegheny Plateau, it begins to warm up and slow its descent. Here smallmouth bass begin to take the place of trout; other warmer water fish such as sunfish and rock bass may be found in slack water and pools.

No. Am. Beaver Spotted Salamander American Redstart Pearly Eye Smallmouth Bass

Piedmont Plateau

Piedmont Plateau

Beaver, red fox, copperhead, black rat snake, spotted salamander or American toad. Birds include the American redstart, Baltimore oriole and the Pileated Woodpecker. Butterflies include the northern pearly eye and zebra swallowtail. Smallmouth bass continues to be the mainstay.

Wildflowers of the C&O Canal

The Canal is a wonderful place to go to enjoy the wildflowers, especially the spring ephemerals. Those are the flowers which make their presence known for a few fleeting weeks and then disappear with virtually no trace. One rather distinctive plant is Dutchman's Breeches (Dicentra cucullaria). They look something like upside-down pantaloons. Look out for a very close relative, a plant called Squirrel Corn (Dicentra canadensis). At first you may think that you're seeing the Dutchman's

Dutchman's Breeches (Dicentra cucullaria)

Bloodroot (Sanguinaria canadensis)

Breeches, but pay close attention and you may see that some of the flowers are not pointed at the top, but rounded. Both of these are close relatives of the Bleeding Heart.

Bloodroot (Sanguinaria canadensis) gets its name from the red juice in its rhizome. This juice was used by Native Americans as a body paint as well as a dye. You can find an extract of Bloodroot

in certain toothpastes. It has a history of medicinal uses though the plant can be toxic. Some of its chemical constituents are being researched as components of possible cancer treatments.

There are places along the canal where

Virginia Bluebells (Mertensia virginica)

Bluebells being overrun by Garlic Mustard (Alliaria petiolata)

wonderful displays of Virginia Bluebells (Mertensia virginica) can be seen. However, the joy of viewing the native spring wildflowers is tempered by the increasing presence of invasive nonnative plants. One of the most prolific is Garlic Mustard (Alliaria petiolata) which is thought to have been introduced to this country by settlers as a food or medicinal plant. One of our rare native butterflies, the West Virginia White Butterfly, is dependent on spring wildflowers called Toothworts as a food source for its caterpillar stage. But the Toothworts are unable to compete with the Garlic Mustard and so the butterfly is also losing ground.

West Virginia White Butterfly (Pieris virginiensis)

Nodding Star of Bethlehem (Ornithogalum nutans)

Cardinal Flower (Lobelia cardinalis)

Another introduced plant which has begun crowding out our diverse native plants along the Canal is the Nodding Star of Bethlehem (Ornithogalum nutans). (The genus means "bird milk.") One of the most spectacular flowers one can see along the river in late summer is the Cardinal Flower (Lobelia cardinalis). Its irregular tubular flowers, with two lobes above and three below, are very attractive to butterflies and hummingbirds, though not to cardinals. Its somewhat less showy cousin, the Great Blue Lobelia (Lobelia syphilitica) can also be found. This plant has a history of medicinal use.

Hibiscus, a very attractive genus, is represented by two different species. The Rose Mallow (Hibiscus moscheutos) as well as the Halberd-leaved Rose Mallow (Hibiscus laevis) can be found at the river's edge at various places.

Great Blue Lobelia (Lobelia syphilitica)

by Kathy Bilton

Plants and Trees of the C&O Canal
and adjacent Potomac River and Public Lands

The C&O Canal is one of the most biologically diverse parks in the National Park system, especially for plant species. The park has recorded over 1,500 species of vascular plants, including over 260 nonnative plant species, over 100 rare, threatened or endangered species of plants in Maryland and The District of Columbia, and one federally endangered plant species. The number of rare plants represents one of the highest concentrations of state-listed rare plants in the eastern U.S. Several species are globally rare, and some occur here because they are dependent upon special habitats and ecological conditions present along the Potomac River.

Numerous ecological factors along the Potomac River create a mosaic of different natural habitats. As the park winds westward from just below the Fall Line to western Maryland, a variety of geologic formations are exposed, supporting diverse native plant communities. Areas along the Potomac River, the Potomac Gorge area for example, are subject to frequent floods, causing canopy gaps, scouring and deposition that creates a diversity of habitats and organisms. Distributions of many northern and southern plant species overlap the Potomac River. Isolated populations of western species survive where rare prairie habitat persists along the river. As a result, rare species occur here that are known in only a few other places in the Mid-Atlantic region, adding to the great diversity of this area.

The Potomac Gorge, with Olmstead Island, Bear Island, and the Billy Goat Trail, is one of the most significant natural areas in the eastern United States. It extends for 15 miles along the Potomac River from Great Falls to Theodore Roosevelt Island, encompassing about 9,700 acres in Virginia, Maryland and the District of Columbia and incorporating sections of C&O Canal and George Washington Memorial Parkway. Because of its unusual hydrogeology, the Gorge is one of the most biologically diverse areas for plant species in particular, serving as a meeting place for northern and southern species, midwestern and eastern species, and mountain and coastal species. The site harbors more than 200 rare species and communities, noteworthy stands of upland forest, many seeps and springs harboring rare groundwater fauna, and abundant wetlands. The National Park Service is the principle landowner in the Gorge. However, The Nature Conservancy co-owns Bear Island in the heart of the Gorge.

Habitats of Rare, Threatened, and Endangered Species
Surveys for RT&E's and unusual biological communities have been conducted by the Maryland Department of Natural Resources Heritage and Biodiversity Conservation Program. Areas with more frequent occurrences of RT&E species and unusual biological communities include portions of Seneca Creek State Park, Great Falls National Park, The C&O National Historical Park, and a large tract of the Greenbriar Branch Watershed; and Cabin John Regional Park, Buck Branch Stream Valley Park, Watts Branch Stream Park, Muddy Branch Stream Park, and Blockhouse Point Conservation Park.

Blockhouse Point Conservation Park is home to one watchlist, one State Threatened, and one State Endangered plant species. In addition, the Conservation Park contains one of the largest undisturbed blocks of forest in the Potomac Subregion, providing habitat for forest interior dwelling bird species. Nine species of threatened, endangered, or watchlist species of plants have been identified in the park along with 39 species of nesting birds.

Rare, Threatened & Endangered Plants of the Upper Potomac

Whorled milkweed   Green dragon   Virg. snakeroot   Asa Gray's sedge   Short's sedge

Chinquapin

Golden-knees

Devil's-bit

Leatherwood   Shooting-star

Honeyvine

Harbinger-of spring   Downey Heuchera

Rose mallow

Spring avens   Green Violet

Leatherflower   Trout lily   Loesel's twayblade   Ostritch fern   Water-ash

Potato dandelion

Rustling wild-petunia

Rustling wild-petunia   Heart-leaved skullcap   Shingle oak

Western Maryland Outfitters and Guides

Guided Nature Tourism experiences are available through commercial guides and outfitters who provide outdoor recreational opportunities for the novice to experienced adventure seeker. Many vendors will even custom design an outdoor experience for you.

Private commercial and nonprofit organizations operate outfitting services in the State of Maryland to provide guided recreational services and rentals on public lands. This listing of outfitters and guides in Western Maryland is provided for your convenience only and is not a recommendation by the State of Maryland or the Maryland Department of Natural Resources to use a specific vendor or service.

Western Maryland Outfitters and Guides Websites
(http://www.dnr.state.md.us/outdooradventures/...)

- AAD Inc., scenic hikes and walks with a professional photographer (.../aad.html)
- A.J's Streamside Services, guided fishing, river wading and streamside camping trips (.../aj.html)
- Advanced Dynamic Therapies, massage and health related therapies (.../dynamic.html)
- Adventure Sports, rock climbing, caving, scuba and snorkeling (.../adventuresports.html)
- Allegany Expeditions, backpacking, canoeing, caving, rock climbing (.../allegany.html)
- Be The Hunted, competitive paintball (.../bethehunted.html)
- Breathe Deep Scuba and Sports, night diving, deep diving, education classes (.../breathe.html)
- Broken Bar Stables, horseback riding, hayrides (.../brokenbar.html)
- Camp Earth, guided wilderness hikes, instructional flatwater kayak tours, nature photo workshops, kids art programs, adventure camps, custom outdoor trips (.../campearth.html)
- Deep Creek Outfitters, ski boat, pontoon and fishing boat rentals (.../dcoutfit.html)
- Grouseland Tours, mountain biking (.../grouseland.html)
- High Mountain Sports, ski, snowboard and m. bike rentals and sales (.../highmtsports.html)
- Hillside Hunting Preserve and Sporting Clays, sporting clays (.../hillside.html)
- Holistic Hiking, guided hikes to improve the mind and body (.../holistic.html)
- Laurel Highlands River Tours, white water rafting, climbing, mountain biking (.../laurel.html)
- Lower Pine Arabians, horseback riding, lessons, training and breeding (.../arabians.html)
- Precision Rafting, white water rafting (.../precision.html)
- River and Trail Outfitters, rafting, canoeing, kayaking, hiking, c-c skiing (.../rtoutfit.html)
- Rocky Gap Lodge and Golf Resort, adventure packages (.../rockylodge.html)
- Savage River Lodge, self-guided orienteering, wildlife walks (.../srlodge.html)
- Smiley's Fun Zone, arcade, miniature golf, bumper boats, batting cages (.../smileys.html)
- Spring Creek Outfitters, fly fishing and bass fishing (.../springcreek.html)
- Upward Enterprises, Inc., rock climbing, caving, kayaking, m. biking, hiking (.../upward.html)
- USA Raft, white water rafting (.../usaraft.html)
- Western Maryland ATV Tours, guided all-terrain vehicle tours (.../atvtours.html)
- Western Maryland Scenic Railroad, steam rail trips (.../railroadhtml)
- Westmar Tours, historic, mystery and seasonal packages (.../westmar.html)

Great Falls Kayaking

At first glance, little has changed in almost 300 years at Great Falls. However, the Falls, once considered deadly beyond measure, have proven navigable for highly skilled whitewater kayakers and canoers, and you will often see kayakers soaring off the drops when the water level is low enough.

In 1975, a trio of boaters including Tom McEwan, Daniel Schnurrenberger, and Wick Walker calculated that they could run the falls safely. After getting permission from the park to be on the falls and taking a vow not to reveal who went first, each plunged over the Virginia side at the primary drop now called the "Spout." Since that first descent, hundreds of boaters have run the Falls, and made thousands of descents.

While running the falls made history and greatly expanded the accepted limits of navigation, that first group was there for another purpose. They were in fact training for a Himalayan expedition to Bhutan. The threesome wanted to determine which rapids they could negotiate at river level with their boats without having to climb around.

Boaters have since explored several other routes down Great Falls. Each includes a combination of an 8-foot drop, a 12-foot drop, and an 18-foot drop, though the order changes depending on whether the boater is running the Virginia side ("U-Hole, S-Turn,& the Spout"), the Maryland side ("Pummel/Sunshine, Z-Turn, Horsehoe), or center ("Grace Under Pressure, Ledge, and Streamers").

In recent years, American Whitewater's volunteers have established a Great Falls Safety Advisory Group with the Park Service, local volunteer fire departments, and regional rescue squads. This group has also worked out a means of communicating with hand signals across the noisy rapids to each other. Boaters have used the system successfully to communicate rescue information to the Park Service's rescue helicopter, the "Eagle."

When I carry my boat down to the Potomac, spectators often ask "Is that safe?" I respond that "If you wear a life jacket, know what you are doing, and have a bombproof kayak roll, then it is relatively safe." In the 24 years since the Falls were first run, there has been one kayaker fatality in 1998, and three notable injuries. In comparison, there have been many fatalities by careless rockhoppers, and fishermen who slipped in above the Falls. As a result, American Whitewater strongly recommends wearing a life jacket.

Jason D. Robertson, American Whitewater

Great Falls Paddlers Agreement
(abridged text from: http://www.americanwhitewater.org/archive/article/2/)

Paul Shelp and Dave Collins, and the American Whitewater's Jason Robertson have reached an informal understanding with authorities for paddling Great Falls. Here is an abridged text:

Boater Etiquette - Great Falls of the Potomac
Boaters should avoid running Great Falls when visitation in the park is high. Morning runs are best. If you must go later in the day, go in a group no larger than four (4) and finish quickly. Never go in a large group, spend excessive time scouting, or carry back up for repeat runs when the park is crowded. Know the hazards of this class 5+ rapid before deciding to run it. Be aware that some of the dangers are not evident, even after careful scouting.

We hope that park rangers, resource managers, and fire and rescue personnel see us not as a potential problem, but as an asset on the water. We can help by warning park visitors engaged in reckless behavior near the banks about the danger of drowning and about the necessity of wearing a life jacket. If a victim does fall into the river, kayakers are in a position to become the "first responder" who gets the victim to shore. If kayakers see other park visitors littering, painting graffiti, or engaging in other harmful, illegal acts, they are encouraged to alert law enforcement immediately.

Montgomery County (Maryland) and Fairfax County (Virginia) fire and rescue squads respond to reported emergencies in the parks or on the river. Both of these rescue squads, as well as C&O Canal NHP rangers, have zodiac-type search and rescue boats and are trained in swift water rescue. The US Park Police "Eagle" helicopter may respond as well.

Kayakers are permitted access to Great Falls from either side of the river across NPS land. However, boaters may not put in above the falls on the Virginia side. You may not put in any higher upstream than the well marked "Fisherman's Eddy" kayak launch site on the Virginia side at Great Falls. On the Maryland side, we are permitted to put in above the falls, and many kayakers prefer this launch site for its relative ease.

The following agreed-upon signals are particularly useful to Potomac boaters:
I AM OK — tap your head with your palm
EMERGENCY — wave both arms (if possible, holding a bright-colored PFD., etc.)
NEED MEDICAL ATTENTION — form an "X" (with arms or other device)

The last two are internationally recognized distress signals. The "I am ok" signal is the most important of all, since it allows the helicopter or zodiac crew to more quickly locate the true emergency, if any.

A major concern related to falls running is large groups running the falls when the park is crowded. It draws park visitors closer to the banks and prompts false alarms to 911. Since 1975, 29 people have drowned at Great Falls. Another concern is boaters getting out of their boats in the midst of the falls and spending excessive time not only scouting, but also walking about, rock-hopping, sunbathing, snacking, wading, etc. Swimming and wading are illegal. Boaters may not swim or wade in the river unless it is necessary due to a wet exit. Boaters should never enter the river without wearing a fastened Personal Floatation Device (PFD). Using and honoring the above guidelines will ensure that Kayaking the Potomac will remain a privilege available to everyone by authority of the County, State, and National Park Service.

Potomac Whitewater Festival
At Great Falls, Maryland

The Potomac Whitewater Festival features a series of dazzling contests requiring kayakers to demonstrate mastery of the fast-moving water near Great Falls on the Potomac River. This three-day whitewater extravaganza is the only event of its kind in the DC area. The competition venue is at Great Falls Park, Virginia. Events ranging from head-spinning rodeo to upstream and downstream sprints to the adrenaline-inducing Great Falls Race are held on the Potomac River at and immediately downriver of Great Falls at the end of May and the beginning of June.

In addition to providing challenge and entertainment for the boaters and spectators, the purpose of the Potomac Whitewater Festival is to raise funds for river conservation and river access in cooperation with the Festival's principal sponsor, American Whitewater. The event schedule is posted in the lower parking lot at Great Falls Park and updated throughout each day.

For more information about the Potomac Whitewater Festival, call: (301) 881-0368.

TEVA 2002 Potomacfest Core Events
Rodeo/Freestyle

This is where boaters can strut their surface boat stuff: wave surfing, enders, pirouettes, cartwheels, retendos, paddle throws, and all other insane Freestyle Moves.

1) Beginner: This category is designed for the entry level paddler interested in freestyle competition. The Beginner level helps the paddler get familiar with paddling in competition. Judging is composed of technical and style only. After placing in the top five in three events over a 1-year period, a Beginner paddler must advance to the Sport category.

2) Sport: This category reflects improved skills and developed strength and stamina. Judging is composed of technical and style only. After placing in the top five in three events over a 1-year period, a Sport paddler must advance to the Expert category.

3) Expert: Competitor skills are high but the format and scoring are less formal than that of the Pro competition. Judging is composed of technical, style, and variety multipliers. Any Expert paddler placing in the top five at three events on the NOWR calendar in a three year period may apply to be upgraded to Pro.

4) Pro NOWR: This showcase event is a professional competition which conforms to NOWR formats and judging rules. Professional boaters who want to earn points towards the 2000 Point Series Championship compete against the best of the best.

http://www.potomacfest.com

Potomac Whitewater Festival
Harpers Ferry, West Virginia

Harpers Ferry is the site of a whitewater kayak race and rodeo. This is an important fund-raiser for the American Whitewater and Save the Blackwater. This event is held 1 mile North West of the Cliffside Inn off Rt. 340, on the right. Please check race information, schedule of events, directions, live entertainment at the festival, and activities for kids.

The KAYAKER OLYMPICS is open to all festival attendees.
There are 6 events in the Kayaker Olympics.

Event #1 - Belly Flop - A huge raft is filled with water and mud. Kayakers must run and belly flop into the raft. This event is judged by the crowd.

Event #2 - Quick Change- Kayakers must strip their street clothes off and don their spray skirt, helmet, and PFD. All paddling gear is covered in ice.

Event #3 - Log Battle - Kayakers battle with padded kayak paddles over two rafts filled with mud.

Event #4 - Big Wheel Drink and Drive- Kayakers must drink one beer before racing their big wheel around the track 3 times. This is a timed event.

Event #5 - Drink and Spin - Kayakers must drink one beer, then spin around 10 times with their head on the handle of a canoe paddle. They must then run 20 yards and repeat this process 3 times.

Event #6 - Boof Gear Challenge - Women contestants only. Put on a Boof Gear over your street clothes then remove their clothing and don a bathing suit and then remove the Boof Gear.

Schedule of Events

This event is sanctioned by the American Canoe Association and you must be a member to participate. Admission to the Festival is $7.00.

Friday:

5:00—9:00	Early Registration. $20.00-Downriver Race, $20-Riot Rodeo, Plus $5-ACA fee

Saturday:

8:30 - 10:AM	Last minute registration and boater check in.
8:30 A.M. - 6:00 P.M.	Canoe and Kayak Swap
11:00 A.M.	Downriver Race Start
1:00 P.M.	Riot Rodeo Start
3:00 P.M.	Festival Start
3:00 - 5:00 P.M.	Live Music
5:00 - 6:00 P.M.	Race & Riot Rodeo Awards
6:00 - 7:00 P.M.	Guide Olympics
7:00 - 8:00 P.M.	Live Auction
8:00 - Midnight	Live Music

Riot Rodeo Entry
Entry fee for the Riot Rodeo is $20.00 before opening and $25.00 after opening. Entry fee for both Riot Rodeo and the Downriver Race is $30.00 before opening and $40.00 after opening.

www.whitewaterfestival.com

Potomac River Smallmouth Bass

The best smallmouth bass fishing lies between Paw Paw, West Virginia and Great Falls, Maryland. There is an untapped brown-bass fishery between Great Falls and Little Falls but there is no access to this portion of the Potomac. Smallmouth bass are dedicated breeders, usually spawning when water temperatures reach 55-60 degrees. Their staple foods are all fish (particularly minnows), crawfish, mayfly, and insects.

The Potomac is made up of shallows, pools, and elevation drops. Everything that lies on the bottom of the river sends a signal to the surface, via the current. Those "signals" are often subtle ripples, and bass live under and around the rocks that form those ripples. Ninety percent of the fish live in ten percent of the water; on almost any sector of the Potomac River there is mostly unproductive water. During the cooler temperatures of spring look for underwater ledges or land points that block the current, thus providing ambush positions for the bass in the area. Standing ledges are great spring habitats, but so are those ledges that are under the surface.

When the water temperature reaches the 50's and slowly continues to rise, it's prespawn-time. Fish are more aggressive and your lure opportunities expand. The lower 50's are best fished with soft plastics, bounced or swum. As the water warms a little, small crawfish-colored crankbaits may be used as can some spinnerbaits—all based on stable water flow. Surface feeding begins at this time of year. Look for pockets of calm water that has current along the perimeter. Buzzbaits, chuggers, poppers and lipped stick baits perform well.

Smallmouth bass will spawn when the water temperature reaches about 60 degrees and the weather is relatively stable. There is a rather lengthily period of inactivity after the spawn, roughly April and also May, sometimes as late as June.

From Seneca to White's Ferry for the early portion of spring, the water warms faster. When this area brings on the spawn, try the Point of Rocks to Knoxville Falls sector. The Lander sector has everything a moving river needs to harbor smallmouth bass. The shore-to-shore above water ledges provide excellent cool-water staging and spawning areas and it's easy to see the more productive fishing holes.

A Winter Hotspot You Need To Try

Smallmouths at the Dickerson Power Plant

A favorite winter time fishing spot is the Dickerson Power Plant discharge on the Potomac River. The warmer discharge water creates an ideal situation for algae and microscopic animal life to grow and thrive. This abundant food source attracts shad, minnows and small fish. These bait fish in turn draw the predator fish, such as bass, stripers, catfish and walleye.

Smallmouth bass and channel catfish congregate at the mouth of the discharge channel, feeding on minnows and crayfish in the warm water. There is a 1/2 mile path from the parking lot to the confluence, where anglers line the bank, casting nightcrawlers, live minnows and small plastic grubs.

December through February is the best time to fish here; the main river must be cold enough to drive the fish into the warm-water plume. The plume of heated water sometimes flows as far as 2.5 miles downstream–down to White's Ferry. The discharge area will be 52-55 degrees and the main river should be close to freezing. It is then that the warm plume is in the near perfect range for smallmouth comfort.

Search for certain types of bottom cover to probe. If the water is raging, the fish will be close to the bottom, out of cover from the direct current. Rocky bottoms are excellent spots. When the water is right, the few proven producers imitate baitfish and crawdads; minnow imitators of four and five-inch Cabin Creek tubes "lubed" with Sticky Liquid work well, and a three-inch grub can be used as a "search" bait. Soak the whole bait with Smelly Jelly crawfish attractant. Allowed these baits to be swept downstream with the current until the pull of a fish is felt.

Where to Catch Fish on the River

The premier game fish from Georgetown to the Potomac is the smallmouth pass. Lures, rubber worms, worms, and live minnows work well; for Carp, doughballs.

The Potomac Gorge and Palisades Mile 0 - 3

Fletcher's Boat House at mile 3.3 is the easiest and safest Potomac River access above Georgetown. shad, herring, white perch, and striped bass are plentiful, especially in spring during the spawning runs.

Chain Bridge upstream to Little Falls Dam Mile 4 - 6

This stretch is good almost year-round, but spring is best. The pools below the dam produce smallmouths.

Little Falls to Stubblefield Falls Mile 6 - 10

Catfish and carp are the mainstay during the warm months, and almost any bait works well. Lazy summer days and the fish are jumpin' . . . Smallmouth that is. Flyfishing off the tips of the small islands can be explosive!

Stubblefield Falls to Old Anglers Inn Mile 10 - 14

The channels between the islands are good for smallmouth, the slower waters are productive for carp and catfish. Violette's Lock, Swain's and Pennyfield locks are convenient parking locations.

Edward's Ferry Mile 30

President Grover Cleveland's favorite fishing site.

White's Ferry Mile 35

Good for crappie and smallmouth year-round but especially in spring and fall. In winter the Dickerson Power Plant warms sections of the River, making the fish active.

Brunswick, Knoxville, and Harpers F. Mile 55 to 61

Very popular for bass fishing. Below Dam 3 is good for catfish and bass. Near Lock 34, the deep channels is productive for crappie, especially in spring and fall.

Snyder's Landing Mile 76-80

The best deepwater bass fishing on the Potomac.

Big Pool and Little Pool Mile 113, 120

These two areas offer the widest variety of fish. Yellow and white perch and crappie are most common.

Maryland Mountain Bike Trails

Green Ridge State Forest, with over 100 miles of dirt roads and trails, stretches across the mountains of western Maryland. Undulating terrain mixes single and doubletrack. A challenging permanent 12-mile mountain bike trail for intermediate to advanced riders has steady climbs, fast down hills, and it is just technical enough. Four easy outs have been located throughout the trail, which offers weary riders a more moderate ride back to the trailhead. The Green Ridge Mountain bike trail map may be obtained from the forest headquarters.

Biking is permitted on all roads within the forest, most of the hiking trail, and on the C&O Canal towpath, which borders the south side. Getting to Green Ridge from Hagerstown, MD: head west on I-68. About 10 miles west of Sideling Hill, exit on to M.V. Smith Road.

Green Ridge State Forest

Trail Type:	Single Track 60%
	Dual Track 40%
Distance:	20.00 miles
Duration:	4 - 5 Hours
Elev. Gain:	750 Feet
Climbing:	Rolling Terrain
Skill Level:	Beginners

Green Ridge State Forest Loop

Nearby City:	Cumberland, MD
Trail Type:	Loop
Distance:	12 total miles
Duration:	2 - 4 hours
Elev. Gain:	1,100 feet
Skill Level:	Difficult

Stafford-East Valley Roads Loop

Nearby City:	Flintstone, MD
Distance:	9 total miles
Trail Type:	Loop

Green Ridge MTB Trail

Nearby City:	Flintstone, MD
Distance:	11.5 total miles
Trail Type:	Loop, Four "easy-outs"
Elev. Gain:	1,000 feet
Skill Level:	Novice to Intermediate
Aerobic:	Very steep hills.
Season:	Avoid hunting season

North of Interstate 68

Nearby City:	Flintstone, MD
Distance:	8 total miles
Trail Type:	Loop
Elev. Gain:	400 feet
Skill Level:	Aerobic: Moderate
Technical:	Easy
Season:	Avoid deer-hunting season.

This eight-mile loop follows well-maintained dirt roads and requires no technical skills. Maps are available at G. R. State Forest headquarters.

Meadow Mountain Trail

Nearby City: Cumberland, Maryland
Distance: 12.00 miles (19.31 KM)
Trail Type: Single Track 50%
Dual Track 30%
Duration: 2 - 3 Hours
Elev. Gain: 750 Feet (229 Meters)
Skill Level: Something for everyone

Stafford-East Valley Roads Loop

Nearby City: Flintstone, MD
Distance: 9 total miles
Trail Type: Loop
Elev. Gain: 1,500 feet
Skill Level: Aerobic: Very difficult
Technical: Easy

Allegany Grove

Nearby City: LaVale, Maryland
Trail Type: Single Track 90%
Dual Track 10%
Distance: 17.00 miles (27.35 KM)
Duration: not specified.
Elev. Gain: 900 Feet (274 Meters)
Skill Level: Intermediate

Follow National Hwy (rt. 40) about 2-3 miles to the stop light. Proceed for about 10 yards from the light and turn into the small gravel lot. Park your car, and ride.

Popular Lick
Meadow Mountain to Popular Lick Loop

This is a long and strenuous 20-mile loop ride for the well-conditioned cyclist. There are rough riding surfaces (mud, rocks, gravel, logs) and many stream crossings. Start early in the day and pack a lunch. Although the trails are well marked, it's a good idea to carry a topo map and compass.

The ride along Meadow Mountain is on a woods road featuring views of the surrounding mountains. The fast descent on Big Run Road is through beautiful forests ending at Big Run State Park, with views of Savage River Reservoir ringed by cliffs and forested hills. The Poplar Lick O.R.V. Trail is a woods road about 5 miles long and has 5 stream crossings. The Three Bridges Trail is a single-track that connects with the Green Trail, an easy woods road that returns you to New Germany State Park.

General location: Five miles southeast of Grantsville, MD.

Elevation change: The loop climbs from 2,468' at New Germany State Park to 2,900' on Meadow Mountain. There's little change in elevation along the ridge until the descent to Big Run Road (2,525'). A gentle descent along the Big Run Road drops you to 1,500' at Savage River Road, followed by a gentle rise up the Savage River and Poplar Lick Run to the starting point in New Germany State Park.

Finding the trail: Take Exit 24 from I-68, follow the signs to New Germany State Park. Phone (301) 895-5453.

Additional Notes:

There are more trails worth exploring at New Germany State Park, and at all other locations given. Seek and explore.

Maryland ORV Trails

Western Maryland offers offroad vehicle trails in three State Forests. All of the trails are open year-round to 4WD / SUV (no permit required), with winter restrictions from December 15 until March 15 on ATV's and motorcycles (permits required) in favor of snowmobiles. The trails in this section may only be used by motorcycles, snowmobiles, and four-wheel vehicles.

Green Ridge State Forest in Allegany County
contact: Green Ridge State Forest, (301) 478-3124

Green Ridge State Forest offers a four-wheel offroad vehicle (ORV) 18-mile loop trail located on East Valley and Stafford Roads. All unregistered motorcycles and four wheelers are required to obtain an identification permit from the Department of Natural Resources. Permits are available from any DNR Regional Service Center or State Forest offices that have designated ORV trails. An Off-Road Vehicle Trail guide that contains useful information and safety recommendations is available from the forest's visitor center. The ORV trail at Green Ridge is located on East Valley Road and Stafford Road.

Potomac-Garrett State Forest in Garrett County
contact: Potomac State Forest, 301-334-9180

Piney Mountain Trail: The Piney Mountain Trail beginning at the San Run-Cranesville Road and ending at the intersection of the Piney Mountain Road and the unnamed dirt road may only be used by: (1) snowmobiles from December 15 through March 15, except during deer firearms season; and (2) two-wheel and four-wheel vehicles the remainder of the year and during the deer firearms season. The western half of the loop may be used by snowmobiles only.

Garrett Trail: That portion of Garrett Trail beginning at Cranesville Road and running south along Snaggy Mountain Road/Hutton-Switch road to the bridge at the head of Herrington Lake may be used only by: (1) snowmobiles from December 15 through March 15, except during deer firearm season; and (2) two-wheel and four-wheel vehicles the remainder of the year and during the deer firearms season. That portion of the Garrett Trail forming the eastern side of the northern loop beginning and ending at the points where the loop leaves the part of the trail running along Snaggy Mountain Road/Hutton-Switch Road, the southern portion of the trail beginning at the bridge at the head of Herrington lake to the trail's end, and the trail connecting at midway the northern loop to the southern portion of the trail may only be used by snowmobiles.

Potomac River Trail: The northern portion of Potomac River Trail beginning at the western boundary of the forest at Rileys Spring Branch and running eastward toward the Potomac River along Laurel Run to the intersection of an unnamed dirt road may be used only by: (1) snowmobiles from December 15 through March 15, except during the deer firearms season; and (2) two-wheel and four-wheel vehicles during the remainder of the year and the deer firearms season.

The eastern portion of the Potomac River Trail beginning at the western boundary of the forest at Rileys Spring Branch and running southward along Audley Riley Road the boundary of the forest near Wallman may be used only by: (1) snowmobiles from December 15 through March 15, except during the firearms season: and (2) two-wheel and four-wheel vehicles during the remainder of the year and during the deer firearms season.

The **western portion of the Potomac River Trail** where it leaves the eastern portion of the trail near the intersection of Audley Riley Road and an unnamed dirt road and running south on and along the access road to the point where the trail ends when it intersects with the southern portion of the trail and the center trail connecting the western and eastern portions which follow the access road may: (1) be used only by snowmobiles from December 15 through March 15.

The **southern portion of the Potomac River Trail** beginning where it intersects with the western portion of the trail and running southward to its intersection with the eastern portion may be used only by snowmobiles, and may not be used by any motorized wheeled vehicle.

Backbone Mountain Trail: That portion of Backbone Mountain Trail beginning near the intersection of Maryland Route 135 and Maryland Route 38 and running northeast to the Juvenile Justice Boy's Camp may only be used by snowmobiles.

That portion of Backbone Mountain Trail beginning near the intersection of Swanton Hill Road and Maryland Route 135 and running northwest in two branches to the Juvenile Justice Boy's Camp and to the boundary line of the forest may be used only by: (1) snowmobiles from December 15 through March 15, except during deer firearms season; and (2) two-wheel and four-wheel vehicles during the remainder of the year and during the deer firearms season.

Savage River State Forest in Garrett County
contact: Savage River State Forest, 301-895-5759
The trails described in this section may only be used by the ORV's indicated.
Park at lot #5, or turn right and park at the administrative office.
The trailhead (Meadow Mountain O.R.V. Trail) is on the right, just past the office.

Meadow Mountain Trail: This trail is great for the first time rider of an ATV. The northern portion of Meadow Mountain trail beginning at and running along East Shale Road (1/4 mile south of U.S. Route 68) southward to the point where it intersects New Germany Road may only be used by: (1) snowmobiles from December 15 through March 15, except during the deer firearm season; and (2) two-wheel and four-wheel vehicles during the remainder of the year.

The **portion of Meadow Mountain Trail** beginning on the southwest side of New Germany Road and running south to Frank Brenneman Road may only be used by snowmobiles.

The **southern portion of Meadow Mountain Trail**, beginning in Deep Creek Lake State Park, lies at the intersection of the Thayerville Fire Tower Road and the State Park Road and running in a northeasterly direction, ending on Compartment 77 may be used by snowmobiles.

Poplar Lick Trail may only be used by motorcycles and four-wheel vehicles. Area prone to flooding. Trail closed during winter months (Jan-Mar). Campsites available - Permit Required.

Margraff Plantation Trail may only be used by: (1) a snowmobile from December 15 through March 15; and (2) two-wheel and four-wheel vehicles during the remainder of the year, except from the end of spring turkey gobbler season to August 15.

Organizations, Clubs, and Groups of the C&O and Potomac River
Offering Nature Programs, Birding Trips, Walks, Hikes, Bikes, and Classes

Adventure Schools Rock Climbing
1-800-39-CLIMB, (301) 263-0900
adventure@adventureschool.com
http://www.adventureschool.com

American Whitewater Affiliation
Nick@amwhitewater.org
http://www.americanwhitewater.org

Appalachian Trail Conference
(304) 535-6331
general@appalachiantrail.org
http://www.appalachiantrail.org

Audubon Naturalist Society
(301) 652-9188
webmaster@audubonnaturalist.org
http://www.audubonnaturalist.org

Baltimore Bird Club
tross@bcpl.net
www.bcpl.net/~tross/baltbird.html

Bike & Brunch, Inc.™
info@bikeandbrunch.com
http://www.bikeandbrunch.com

Blur Ridge Bycycle Club, Inc.
bike@roava.net
www.roava.net/~bike/index.html

C&O Canal association
http://www.candocanal.org

Canal Cruisers Association
http://www.ccadc.org

Center Hiking Club
dmaidt@smart.net
http://www.smart.net/~dmaidt/
chc_presletr.html

CHAOS
(410)349-3953
http://jenzakayaker.tripod.com

Chesap. Hiking & Outdoor Society
River & Trail Outfitters
888-I GO PLAY, (301) 695-5177
river@rivertrail.com
http://www.rivertrail.com

Chesapeake Mountain Bike Club
of Central Maryland
cmbc_info@annapolis.net
http://www.annapolis.net/cmbc

Cumberland Valley Cycling
Clubcjo1329@cs.com
http://pilot.wash.lib.md.us/cvcc

Dave Brown's Canoeing Adventures
(703) 281-4380
canoeadventures@mindspring.com
http://canoeadventures.
home.mindspring.com/

Friends of the Potomac
(202) 467-4000
info@potomacfriends.org

Interstate Commission on the
Potomac River Basin
http://www.
potomacriver.org/Calendar.htm

Mark Kovach Fishing Services
dmkfs@erols.com
http://www.mkfs.com

Maryland Dep. of Natural Resources
Conservation Education Programs
http://www.dnr.state.md.us/
education/educators.html

Maryland Native Plant Society
MNPS@toad.net
http://www.mdflora.org

The Monocacy Canoe Club
http://www.monocacycanoe.org

The Nature Conservancy
(800) 628-6860
comment@tnc.org
http://nature.org

Pedalers Touring Club
pptcinfo@netscape.net
http://www.bikepptc.org

Potomac Appalachian Trail Club
(703) 242-0693
info@patc.net
http://www.patc.net/index.htm

Potomac Conservancy
(703) 276-2777
webmaster@potomac.org
http://www.potomacconservancy.org

PotomacPaddlesports.com, Inc.
1-877-529-2542, 301-515-7337

info@potomacpaddlesports.com
http://www.
potomacpaddlesports.com

Potomac Pedalers Touring Club
pptcinfo@netscape.net
http://www.bikepptc.org

The Potomac River Guide
http://www.mindspring.
com/~riverguide/pot085.htm

Potomac River Smouth Club
Webmaster@PRSC.ORG
http://prsc.org/club.htm

Potomac Valley Audubon Society
http://www.potomacaudubon.
org/index.html

Riverbend Nature Center
Great Falls, VA 22006
Phone: 703.759.3211

Sierra Club Maryland Chapter
(301) 277-7111
laurel.imlay@sierraclub.org
http://maryland.sierraclub.org

Terrapin Trail Club
pdo@ttc.umd.edu
http://www.
ttc.umd.edu/resources/mtb.html

Trout Unlimited
Nat Cap Chapter
webmaster@tu-ncc.org

Virginia Native Plant Society
vnpsofc@shentel.net
http://www.vnps.org

Washington Area Bicyclist Asso.
(202) 628-2500, waba@waba.orghttp:/\
www.waba.org

Washington Area Butterfly Club
http://users.sitestar.net/butterfly/

Washington Canoe Club
wcanoe@wcanoe.org
http://www.wcanoe.org

Washington Women Outdoors
(301) 864-3070, wwo@patriot.net
washingtonwomenoutdoors.org

Index

Discovering the Index |